POPE FRANCIS

Fratelli Tutti

On Fraternity
and Social Friendship

Introduction by

DANIEL P. HORAN, OFM

ORBIS BOOKS
Maryknoll, New York 10545

Copyright © 2020 by Libreria Editrice Vaticana 00120 Città del Vaticano.

Published in 2020 by Orbis Books.
Introduction © 2020 by Daniel P. Horan, OFM.

Manufactured in the United States of America.
Book design and typesetting by Joan Weber Laflamme.

Library of Congress Control Number: 2020947756

CONTENTS

Introduction   v
Daniel P. Horan, OFM

**Encyclical Letter *Fratelli Tutti* of the Holy Father
   Francis on Fraternity and Social Friendship**   1

   Chapter One
   Dark Clouds over a Closed World   5

   Chapter Two
   A Stranger on the Road   26

   Chapter Three
   Envisaging and Engendering an Open World   39

   Chapter Four
   A Heart Open to the Whole World   57

   Chapter Five
   A Better Kind of Politics   69

   Chapter Six
   Dialogue and Friendship in Society   91

   Chapter Seven
   Paths of Renewed Encounter   102

   Chapter Eight
   Religions at the Service of Fraternity in Our World   124

INTRODUCTION

DANIEL P. HORAN, OFM

During the last years of his life, Saint Francis of Assisi (ca. 1182–1226) traveled to various communities of his brother friars. Having already stepped down from leadership as the general minister of the Franciscan order in 1221, these last years were marked by both his declining health and a persistent desire to preach the gospel, particularly in a manner that challenged his fellow friars to return continually to the basics of the *vita evangelica*—the "gospel life"—which is the fundamental vocation that every baptized Christian shares and to which members of the Franciscan community had promised lifelong obedience.

We know from his writings and subsequent scholarship that Saint Francis wished to address his brother friars on topics related to two areas of concern that troubled him during these last years of his life. The first was internal, namely, that he wanted to exhort them to hold true to the essence of their calling, which *Il Poverello* regularly summarized as both "to live the Holy Gospel" and "to walk in the footprints of our Lord Jesus Christ."[1] He was always concerned that his brothers, and all Christian women and men, focus on their primary responsibility, which is to live more like Christ in all that they do.

Daniel P. Horan, OFM, is a Franciscan friar and Duns Scotus Professor of Spirituality at Catholic Theological Union in Chicago.

[1] For example, see Francis of Assisi, "The Earlier Rule," 1.1; "The Later Rule," 1.1; and "The Testament," no. 14; in *Francis of Assisi: Early Documents*, ed. Regis J. Armstrong, J. A. Wayne Hellmann, and William J. Short, 3 vols. (New York: New City Press, 1999–2001), 1:63–64, 100, and 125, respectively. Hereafter cited as *FAED*.

The second concern was external. Saint Francis was well aware of the shifting social, cultural, and ecclesial dynamics of his time. The early thirteenth century was a tumultuous moment in history. Describing these shifts, especially in the centuries and decades immediately preceding the birth of the Franciscan movement, the Italian historian Giacomo Todeschini writes: "From 1000 to 1200, Western Europe grew in many ways. The inhabitants of cities and countryside multiplied, more land was cultivated, the income of landowners grew and the amount of goods in circulation increased." Reflecting on the consequences of these changes, he adds, "In the cities, families strong enough to command grew in number, while the territorial aristocrats looked for any way to turn their de facto power into a perpetual government. Struggles for power—small and large—became a daily practice."[2]

With increased concentrations of wealth and power in the hands of fewer people in society, Saint Francis was concerned about the ways the shifting political and economic dynamics of the time were affecting those most vulnerable in his community—the poor, the infirm, the outcasts. A large part of his own conversion experience was tied to recognizing that another way to live was possible, and that the pattern for this alternative way of life was the gospel. This conviction about the central purpose of Christianity as the pattern for another way to be in the world led him to speak in exhortatory tones and in a manner reflecting great urgency.

Saint Francis preached this message throughout his life, and he did so in both word and deed. But it is one recorded instance of such an appeal to his friar brothers, preached sometime between 1223 and his death in 1226, that would inspire a pope centuries later; a pope who was so captivated by the story and example of this saint from Assisi that he would take the saint's name for

---

[2] Giacomo Todeschini, *Franciscan Wealth: From Voluntary Poverty to Market Society*, trans. Donatella Melucci (St. Bonaventure, NY: Franciscan Institute Publications, 2009), 11.

his own. This pope, witnessing comparable social, political, and economic upheaval early in the twenty-first century, would renew the message proclaimed by Saint Francis and admonish his sisters and brothers throughout the world to remember that Jesus Christ had called all of us to live another way.

On the feast day of Saint Francis of Assisi, October 4, 2020, Pope Francis issued the encyclical *Fratelli Tutti*, which is an Italian translation of the opening Latin words (*omnes fratres*, "all brothers" or "all of us, brothers") of Saint Francis's "Admonition VI." Originally delivered within the context of an all-male audience of Franciscan friars (hence the gender-exclusive construction, "all *brothers*"), the message continues to speak through the ages. Retrieved by Pope Francis as a summary theme for the 287-paragraph-long document that followed, the title aimed to remind contemporary people that we are "all brothers and sisters" to one another, regardless of whatever distinctions or differences we may have or that society imposes on others. It was in the spirit of Saint Francis's original admonition, one that exhorted his brothers to follow Christ and not shy away from the consequences of genuine Christian discipleship, that the pope exercised his universal magisterial authority in addressing all modern women and men. Saint Francis's original admonition reads:

> Let all of us, brothers, consider the Good Shepherd Who bore the suffering of the cross to save His sheep.
>
> The Lord's sheep followed Him in tribulation and persecution, in shame and hunger, in weakness and temptation, and in other ways; and for these things they received eternal life from the Lord.
>
> Therefore, it is a great shame for us, the servants of God, that the saints have accomplished great things and we want only to receive glory and honor by recounting them.[3]

---

[3] Francis of Assisi, "Admonition VI," 1–3, in *FAED*, 1:131.

Although the full text of this original admonition does not appear in its entirety in *Fratelli Tutti*, the general theme of the message rings true throughout the encyclical: it is a call to action, an exhortation to renewal, an invitation to embrace ongoing conversion. As the Franciscan scholar Robert Karris notes in his commentary on "Admonition VI," the challenge of the message is a kind of wake-up call to complacent Christians who uncritically assume that merely going to church once a week or identifying as a Christian is sufficient. On the contrary, Saint Francis expresses his concern that we do not heed the gospel imperative to live another way. Expounding on this, Karris writes: "Jesus did this; the saints followed his good example. Surely, they present us with much to imitate in our religious lives. And in all honesty, what do we do? We sit around and talk about the examples, or just preach about them from the pulpit, or tell them to students in the classroom. Indeed, shame on us!"[4]

Just as the changing circumstances of Saint Francis's time were leading to increased suffering and inequality, so too we face unprecedented challenges in our own time, but on a greater global scale. Published in the midst of the COVID-19 pandemic, dramatic rises in economic inequality, increasingly overt racism and xenophobia, violence in all corners of the world, and the existential threat of global climate change, *Fratelli Tutti* takes as its starting point the need to name and respond to what Vatican II called in *Gaudium et Spes* "the signs of our times" and to do so in the "light of the Gospel" (no. 4). The starting point and guiding principle for this renewal is what we might call a Franciscan vision of the world, which is shared across the centuries by both men named Francis and is present throughout *Fratelli Tutti*.

---

[4] Robert J. Karris, OFM, *The Admonitions of Saint Francis: Sources and Meanings* (St. Bonaventure, NY: Franciscan Institute Publications, 1999), 92.

The Franciscan Tradition in Pope Francis's Worldview

While this is technically Pope Francis's third encyclical letter— the first was *Lumen Fidei* (2013), the second was *Laudato Si'* (2015)—this is only the second that carries the singular weight of his distinctive pastoral vision, since the drafting of the first encyclical actually began under Pope Benedict XVI's direction and was later completed by Pope Francis. This is a significant detail because it highlights the continuity of the Franciscan tradition's influence throughout Pope Francis's writings, ministry, and worldview. "Francis inspired these pages," said the pope about Saint Francis of Assisi in the opening section of *Fratelli Tutti*. Recalling that Saint Francis inspired the pope to write his last encyclical letter in 2015, *Laudato Si' (On Care for Our Common Home)*, Pope Francis situates this current teaching document again within the framework of Franciscan spirituality and theology. He also traveled to Assisi to commemorate the feast of Saint Francis and officially sign this new encyclical on the feast day of Saint Francis.

While there are many avenues we might explore that highlight the pope's Franciscan inspiration, it is worthwhile to look at four central themes arising from Saint Francis and the Franciscan tradition that inform and guide *Fratelli Tutti*.[5]

The concept of fraternitas

The English translation of the Latin term *fraternitas* as "fraternity" has garnered criticism, even before the encyclical was published.[6] Understandably, the commonsense interpretation of

---

[5] Some of the following section appeared in an earlier form in Daniel P. Horan, "Relationship Leads Us to Peace: Three Key Franciscan Themes in 'Fratelli Tutti,'" *National Catholic Reporter* (October 4, 2020).

[6] For example, see Daniel P. Horan, "The Origin and Context of Pope Francis's Forthcoming Encyclical Title," *Medium* (September 5, 2020); Phyllis Zagano, "'Fratelli tutti' Does Not Include Women, and Neither Does 'Fraternity,'" *National Catholic Reporter* (September 21, 2020); and Joshua J.

the term views the concept as exclusively masculine, referring to the "bond among brothers" or "brotherhood." Indeed, this is an accurate understanding, particularly when one considers that the term is most often used in the contemporary context of the United States in reference to male college students belonging to exclusive social organizations that often emphasize a party lifestyle.

However, the term takes on a slightly different and notably significant meaning when viewed through the lens of the Franciscan theological tradition. It carries at least two senses in this context. The first is not that unlike the reference to college social organizations, albeit without the implications of Bacchanalia. Dating back to Saint Francis himself, whenever the Franciscan friars refer to their local communities of men religious, the term used has been *fraternity*. It is also a term that is used by the Secular Franciscan Order in reference to the local communities or associations of women and men who have professed to live according to the Franciscan Rule in their respective secular contexts. In this way *fraternity* takes on a rather practical meaning, serving as the term for a particular group of Franciscans.

The second sense of *fraternitas* also goes back to Saint Francis himself, and it is more theological than it is practical. *Fraternity* in this sense is more expansive and has to do with the kind of relationship one has with another. The reason that Saint Francis preferred the title "brother" was simple: he truly meant that he saw himself as inherently related to all men and women, and even nonhuman creatures as part of God's one family of creation. To talk about fraternity as a disposition or value is to talk about how you view and relate to other people, including strangers and those who may be very different from you. It is about recognizing intrinsic familial ties with all people and creatures.

McElwee, "Catholic Women Criticize 'Mansplaining' of Pope's Masculine Encyclical Title," *National Catholic Reporter* (September 24, 2020).

Pope Francis picks up on the Franciscan logic of *fraternitas* in the third chapter of *Fratelli Tutti*. He critiques societal relationships determined by affinity, preferences, status, or any other feature, and argues for a more fundamental concept of human relationship: fraternity. "Fraternity is born not only of a climate of respect for individual liberties, or even of a certain administratively guaranteed equality. Fraternity necessarily calls for something greater, which in turn enhances freedom and equality" (no. 103).

Earlier in chapter two of the encyclical, the pope uses the parable of the good Samaritan (Lk 10:25–37) to show how the Christian notion of relationship with others transcends the limits and qualifications we are quick to use in isolating ourselves from solidarity with others. By contrast, if we recognize that we are all sisters and brothers to one another, then we have an inherent bond with one another that demands something of us—our love, respect, and care. Pope Francis highlights the demands that a spirit of fraternity places on us in relationship to one another in human society. The pope says that "we are constantly tempted to ignore others, especially the weak." He notes that "for all the progress we have made, we are still 'illiterate' when it comes to accompanying, caring for, and supporting the most frail and vulnerable members of our developed societies. We have become accustomed to looking the other way, passing by, ignoring situations until they affect us directly" (no. 64).

Saint Francis instructed his followers that what it meant to live the Christian life according to his distinctive vision basically boils down to "walking in the footprints of our Lord Jesus Christ," a phrase that appears throughout his writings. Living like Jesus means prioritizing relationship above all else; it means caring for those in need, regardless of their identity or what affiliations they might have. Pope Francis lifts this up as not only something reserved for Franciscan friars and sisters, but also for all human beings, who are fundamentally interdependent and connected to one another. How we think of ourselves in relationship to others ought to be governed by this principle of our a priori interrelatedness as sisters and brothers. And the way we form our worldviews, make decisions, engage in the public square, and interact with one another at all levels should be grounded in our inextricable *fraternitas* with all.

The Franciscan notion of poverty and relationship to property

I remember once giving a talk to a group of students from a religious order in the northeastern United States. The director of formation had invited me to give a presentation on the theme of Franciscan spirituality. I prepared my remarks, keeping in mind how limited my time was, and arrived to give my hour-long talk. I covered the fundamentals of the Franciscan worldview, explained briefly Saint Francis's own experience of ongoing conversion, and highlighted the ways the Franciscan tradition has sought over the centuries to renew our commitment to following Christ by living the gospel as genuinely as possible. When I was finished speaking and opened the floor for questions and discussion, the priest who had invited me to speak made the first comment. He expressed gratitude for what I had shared but also puzzlement. He had come to the presentation expecting "to hear a lot more about poverty, since isn't that what you Franciscans love so much?"

My response was swift, because I had encountered this sort of assumption about the Franciscan tradition before (if it's not poverty, then it's almost always about the saint's love of animals). I explained that I had talked about the Franciscan notion of poverty the whole time, emphasizing repeatedly the absolute primacy of relationship in Saint Francis's worldview informed by the gospel. What this priest was expecting was to hear something more banal, something more in keeping with some kind of praise for abject material poverty as an end in itself. It was then that I took the opportunity to introduce the basic fact that Franciscans do not actually profess a vow of poverty, but rather a vow to live *sine proprio*, a Latin phrase that means "without anything of one's own."

Saint Francis, like Jesus of Nazareth long before him, did not see material poverty—that lack of the basic things necessary for human flourishing, like food, water, shelter, love, healthcare, clothing, and so on—as something to be praised or desired. Abject poverty is an evil, whereby people are forced into terribly dehumanizing circumstances. Christians and all people of good will should fight to eliminate it and liberate people from such conditions. But Saint Francis came to recognize that possessiveness—of both material goods and nonmaterial attitudes, prejudices, and hubris—inevitably get in the way of authentic human relationships. The amassing of property and the appropriating of power, and especially the effort to maintain or increase those two things, creates distance between people. Walls are erected, lines drawn, and persons isolated against the real or perceived threat other people present to those who wish to maintain their control over their possessions.

For Saint Francis, *sine proprio* was never understood as an end itself, but rather as a means to a more important and foundational end: *relationship*.[7] The Franciscan tradition teaches that evangelical poverty is about living more like Christ, which ought to inform how one views oneself, others, and the world. Pope Francis picks up on this theme in *Fratelli Tutti* from the outset, noting how contemporary society encourages a particular way of living, one that promotes individual accumulation of wealth, property, and power for its own sake. As he notes in chapter one of the encyclical, this has rendered our modern societies more unequal, more fearful, and more isolated (nos.

---

[7] For more on the history of this Franciscan theme, see Michael F. Cusato, "The Renunciation of Power as a Foundational Theme in Early Franciscan History," in *The Early Franciscan Movement (1205–1239): History, Sources, and Hermeneutics* (Spoleto: Centro Italiano di Studi sull'Alto Medioevo, 2009), 29–48; Michael F. Cusato, "The Early Franciscans and the Use of Money," in *Poverty and Prosperity: Franciscans and the Use of Money*, ed. Daria Mitchell (St. Bonaventure, NY: Franciscan Institute Publications, 2009), 13–38; and Jacques Dalarun, *Francis of Assisi and Power*, trans. Anne Bartol (St. Bonaventure, NY: Franciscan Institute Publications, 2007).

22–29). His turn in chapter two toward the Lukan parable of the good Samaritan offers an illustration of this alternative— Christian, Franciscan—worldview in practice. Whereas others walking past the man injured by robbers would not allow themselves to move beyond the figurative walls of their own comfort, the Samaritan did not allow anything, including differences in ideology or religious perspective, to get in the way of attending to the needs of the other. In this way *fraternitas* is modeled by the decision to voluntarily surrender property (the money given and promised to the innkeeper), as well as comfort, convenience, and time in order to be a true brother to another human being in need.

Throughout the rest of the encyclical Pope Francis returns to this theme of *fraternitas* in action as marked by an attitude of *sine proprio*. He critiques those individuals and nations that jealously protect access to their borders, which is a form of turning away from migrants and refugees in order to maintain the status quo. Citing his earlier encyclical *Laudato Si'*, the pope states in chapter three that "the Christian tradition has never recognized the right to property as absolute or inviolable, and has stressed the social purpose of all forms of private property." Pope Francis adds, referencing John Paul II's 1981 encyclical *Laborem Exercens*, "The principle of the common use of created goods is the 'first principle of the whole ethical and social order'; it is a natural and inherent right that takes priority over others" (no. 120). This is deeply Franciscan in spirit because it makes plain that the common good supersedes any claim to individual property, especially when so few have so much while so many lack the most basic goods. The later chapters return again and again tacitly to this Franciscan view of property and the common good, outlining a clear vision for how the principle of solidarity demands another way of relating to others. For example, in chapter six the pope speaks at great length about the need to develop a "culture of encounter" that is uninhibited by prejudices, fear, and cultural chauvinism.

A culture of encounter: Crossing borders, building bridges

Early in the document the pope recalls Saint Francis's famous encounter with Sultan Malik-el-Kamil at Damietta, Egypt, in 1219.[8] Drawing a connection to that historic episode of mutual respect, peacemaking, and fraternity—a shared sense of a fraternal bond between the two men from different cultures and religions—Pope Francis identified a comparable sense of encounter he had with Grand Imam Ahmad Al-Tayyeb, whom he met in Abu Dhabi in 2019. At that meeting the two religious leaders signed a document, "Human Fraternity for World Peace and Living Together," which included the shared assertion that "God has created all human beings equal in rights, duties, and dignity, and has called them to live together as brothers and sisters."[9]

The nod to the importance of interreligious dialogue and friendship across differences in the global effort to promote human solidarity is no small gesture. Pope Francis, taking seriously the prioritization of fraternal and sororal relationship with all people modeled by Saint Francis, describes this social teaching as directed not only to his Christian sisters and brothers, but also addressed to all people of good will. This expansive audience reflects the inclusive vision articulated at the outset of *Laudato Si'* and encyclicals of his predecessors, dating back to John XXIII's 1963 document *Pacem in Terris*, which was geared not only to Catholics and other Christians but also all people of good will.

Saint Francis is known to have crossed many borders and built many bridges in his time. He intentionally transgressed the

---

[8] For more on this encounter, see George Dardess and Marvin L. Krier Mich, *In The Spirit of Saint Francis and The Sultan: Catholics and Muslims Working Together for the Common Good* (Maryknoll, NY: Orbis Books, 2011); and Paul Moses, *The Saint and the Sultan: The Crusades, Islam, and Francis of Assisi's Mission of Peace* (New York: Doubleday, 2009).

[9] Pope Francis and Grand Imam Ahmad Al-Tayyeb, "Human Fraternity for World Peace and Living Together," February 4, 2019.

social, civil, and ecclesial borders of his community to embrace and then live with lepers who had been ostracized from the ordinary life of Assisi. He crossed the border of the Fifth Crusade's battle to engage in a peaceful encounter and exchange of ideas with the sultan, despite the vilification of Muslims by the majority of Christian Europe at the time, including and especially by Pope Innocent III. He even moved across the border of species when he sincerely referred to nonhuman creatures as his sisters and brothers, recognizing that lines of demarcation between the human and nonhuman are in some ways artificial constructs, given our interdependence on one another and universal reliance on our common source, which is God.

Today Pope Francis calls on all his brothers and sisters, regardless of their religious tradition or nation of origin, to "see things in a new light and to develop new responses" to the challenges before us (no. 128). Among these challenges is the increasing tendency that individuals and nations have to erect borders and walls, literal and figurative ones, which separate, isolate, and exclude the most vulnerable in our world. Pope Francis's consistent critiques throughout the encyclical of consumerism, capitalism, nationalism, xenophobia, and other ascendant ideologies of our time also gesture to the importance of bridge building between peoples.

The pope points to love as the necessary ground for our building a "culture of encounter," which "means that we, as a people, should be passionate about meeting others, seeking points of contact, building bridges, planning a project that includes everyone" (no. 216). He speaks throughout *Fratelli Tutti* of the evils of apathy and indifference, a recurring theme in his preaching and magisterial teaching. These attitudes not only prevent us from the capacity for compassion—the ability to suffer with others in solidarity—but they also promote an individualism that creates separation and prohibits authentic relationship. What results is not only social division, but also tremendous suffering, which is felt most acutely by the poor and vulnerable.

The imposition of physical and ideological borders does great harm to human dignity, particularly for migrants and immigrants, which is why Pope Francis strongly emphasizes the need for "fraternal gratuitousness" or the building of bridges to a better life for those who suffer the most without asking the costs (no. 140). This is only possible, the pope notes, if we measure ourselves not merely as one country competing against others, but "as part of the larger human family." He adds: "Only a social and political culture that readily and 'gratuitously' welcomes others will have a future" (no. 141). It is only in the spirit of Saint Francis's *fraternitas* that such reforms can take place.

Peacemaking and reconciliation

Toward the end of *Fratelli Tutti*, Pope Francis writes: "In many parts of the world, there is a need for paths of peace to heal open wounds. There is also a need for peacemakers, men and women prepared to work boldly and creatively to initiate processes of healing and renewed encounter" (no. 225). Here he again embodies the wisdom of Saint Francis as a promoter of peacemaking and reconciliation.

Remembered as a faithful reformer of the church and society, Saint Francis's commitment to peacemaking and reconciliation as the means for reforming dysfunctional relations between people was grounded in his understanding of universal *fraternitas*—that we are all brothers and sisters to one another and ought to act like it. In his famous "Canticle of the Creatures," Saint Francis barely mentions human beings. When he does, toward the end of the text, after invoking many other aspects of creation, he says that we humans are most authentically in keeping with God's intention for us when we "give pardon," "bear infirmity and tribulation," and "endure in peace."[10]

---

[10] Francis of Assisi, "Canticle of the Creatures," in *FAED* 1:113–14.

Similarly, Pope Francis stresses the need for another kind of being in the world, one that is more human, one that returns to this foundational vocation wherein God calls all people to be peacemakers and reconcilers. Returning to the Franciscan principle of *fraternitas*, the pope invokes the family as a metaphor for reimagining social structures and political engagement. He notes that families regularly have disputes, but the way that healthy families resolve them can be a model for thinking about the bigger picture of human dynamics in society.

> They may quarrel, but there is something that does not change: the family bond. Family disputes are always resolved afterwards. The joys and sorrows of each of its members are felt by all. That is what it means to be a family! If only we could view our political opponents or neighbors in the same way that we view our children or spouse, mother or father! How good would this be! (no. 230)

Authentic peacemaking requires truth telling and a shared commitment to the good of the other.[11] It also requires recognizing how decisions have consequences—sometimes dramatically negative ones—for "the more vulnerable members of society" (no. 234). He adds: "Those who work for tranquil social coexistence should never forget that inequality and lack of integral human development make peace impossible" (no. 235). Again, this harkens back to the model and vision of Saint Francis, who, in promoting *fraternitas* as the lens through which to view all relationships, always prioritized the poor and marginalized.

---

[11] For more on peacemaking and reconciliation, see Robert J. Schreiter, *Reconciliation: Mission and Ministry in a Changing Social Order* (Maryknoll, NY: Orbis Books, 1992); Robert J. Schreiter, *The Ministry of Reconciliation: Spirituality and Strategies* (Maryknoll, NY: Orbis Books, 1998); Eli S. McCarthy, ed., *A Just Peace Ethic Primer: Building Sustainable Peace and Breaking Cycles of Violence* (Washington, DC: Georgetown University Press, 2020).

Pope Francis, like his medieval namesake, does not condone "easy" forgiveness or reconciliation, which often comes at the expense of silencing or dismissing the discomfiting experiences and histories of those who have been victimized. Instead, he insists on the importance of memory in a manner evoking the theological concept "dangerous memory" of the late German theologian Johann Baptist Metz, and the rejection of decisions or actions arising from "fear and resentment" (no. 266).[12] In the final chapter of the encyclical the pope appeals to all religious believers, regardless of their tradition, to be agents of reconciliation, recognizing the fundamental commitment we all have to promote the common good.

Speaking from the Christian perspective, Pope Francis ties together the importance of the example of Jesus Christ and *fraternitas* as the foundation for our universal human vocation to be peacemakers and reconcilers. "For us the wellspring of human dignity and fraternity is in the Gospel of Jesus Christ. From it, there arises, for Christian thought and for the action of the Church, the primacy given to relationship, to the encounter with the sacred mystery of the other, to universal communion with the entire human family, as a vocation of all" (no. 277).

These four themes offer but a taste of the robust Franciscan inspiration discernable throughout *Fratelli Tutti* and in the life and ministry of Pope Francis. While a whole volume could be written on the distinctive Franciscan character of this and the pope's other writings, I want to move now to offer a brief reading guide to the encyclical, highlighting along the way significant points worth looking for as you explore the text.

A Brief Reading Guide to *Fratelli Tutti*

While Saint Francis and the Franciscan tradition offer the inspirational impetus for *Fratelli Tutti*, Pope Francis uses this

---

[12] See Johann Baptist Metz, *Faith in History and Society: Toward a Practical Fundamental Theology*, trans. J. Matthew Ashley (New York: Crossroad Publishing, 2011).

occasion to draw the world's attention to numerous challenges, crises, and threats that exist before us today. The overarching focus of the encyclical is to invite readers to remember that another way of being in the world and structuring our societies is possible, and the framework for that alternative worldview is found in the gospel of Jesus Christ. In a manner similar to, but not as structurally obvious as, *Laudato Si'*, Pope Francis engages in a "see, judge, act" model of translating the church's social teachings into praxis.[13] Within the Catholic Church this model was first articulated in 1961 by Pope John XXIII in his encyclical *Mater et Magistra*, which outlined how the baptized can take the principles we hold as essential to our faith and put them into practice. Near the end of the text, in a section keenly titled "Practical Suggestions," he writes:

> There are three stages which should normally be followed in the reduction of social principles into practice. First, one reviews the concrete situation; secondly, one forms a judgment on it in the light of these same principles; thirdly, one decides what in the circumstances can and should be done to implement these principles. These are the three stages that are usually expressed in the three terms: look, judge, act. (no. 236)

Because of the number of chapters (a short introduction plus eight chapters) and the organization of the document (unlike *Laudato Si'*, this encyclical does not map evenly onto the threefold structure), the "see, judge, act" framework is not as intuitive in the outline of *Fratelli Tutti*, but it is operative in the text all the same.

Pope Francis opens the document with a short introduction that outlines the major theme of the text: *fraternitas* as inspired by the legacy of Saint Francis of Assisi. He then moves to

---

[13] For an overview of this approach, see Erin M. Brigham, *See, Judge, Act: Catholic Social Teaching and Service Learning*, rev. ed. (Winona, MN: Anselm Academic, 2019), 23–31.

chapter one, in which the "seeing" work unfolds. Here we get an accurate, if at times sad, depiction of the current state of world affairs. In his social analysis the pope notes that there is increased inequality, division and polarization, dehumanizing of certain populations, and a rise in the instrumentalizing of human beings who are "sacrificed" and "discarded." The wealth gap means that fewer and fewer people and communities are holding most of the world's wealth, while the vast majority of the global population barely survives. Furthermore, growing individualism and indifference—themes that repeatedly appear in the pope's writings and preaching—have led to widespread apathy in the face of unimaginable suffering, especially in the age of the novel coronavirus pandemic. Pope Francis summarizes what he sees with the line: "We are more alone than ever in an increasingly massified world that promotes individual interests and weakens the communitarian dimension of life" (no. 12). Something has to change.

Having outlined some of the key signs of our times, Pope Francis turns to the gospel parable of the good Samaritan (Lk 10:25–37) as one source for "judging" the circumstances in which we find ourselves as outlined in the previous chapter. The reference to this parable is an echo of one of Pope Francis's earliest pastoral visits to the small island of Lampedusa, Italy, in July 2013. In his address then, the pope used the parable of the good Samaritan to frame his remarks and draw greater attention to the "globalized indifference" that results in the unnecessary deaths of thousands of migrants and refugees.[14] This is a beautiful reflection in which the pope presents a detailed exegesis and application of this otherwise familiar gospel passage. He draws out the parallels to our time and the challenges that people of good will face when confronted with those whom we can assist or ignore, just like the man left on the side of the road by robbers. In true Pope Francis form, he highlights in this encyclical key themes that resonate through the centuries: the persistence

---

[14] Pope Francis, "Homily of Holy Father Francis: Visit to Lampedusa," July 8, 2013.

of indifference; societies that exclude the weak; and political movements that promote selfishness, individualism, and apathy. Jesus's message in the parable continues to challenge us today and provides us with an appropriate lens through which to interpret the signs of our times outlined in chapter one.

The remaining chapters, three through eight, cover a tremendous amount of ground. Many of the topics the pope engages in these chapters will be familiar to those well versed in the holy father's homilies, addresses, and writings. It's notable that many of the references throughout these sections are to previous addresses or texts by Pope Francis, which shows how this particular encyclical fits comfortably within the pope's own theological, social, and pastoral outlook and ministry. What we see in these chapters is a presentation of what the world *could be* if we took the gospel seriously and allowed the model of Christ's life, death, and resurrection to inform how we relate to one another and structure our communities. This includes an emphasis on openness to the other, which requires each of us having an "open heart" (chapter four) and the promotion of an "open world" (chapter three) in which all people are at home and treated as sisters and brothers to one another (*fraternitas*).

Chapters five and six build on these foundational understandings of openness and outline what these might look like in practice. For example, chapter five centers on the creation of what Pope Francis calls "a better kind of politics" (no. 154). This political worldview ought to be shaped by the prioritization of the common good, whereas so much of the contemporary political scene—all over the world—is dominated by individualism, xenophobia, unchecked capitalism, and other deleterious trends that appeal to the basest fears of populations. Instead, the pope calls for "political love," a startling phrase in an age of such partisan division, but one that summarizes well the truth that "charity is at the heart of every healthy and open society" (no. 184). Chapter six builds on this political philosophy, making clear that such a political framework can only take root if we are committed to "dialogue and friendship in society." At the outset of the chapter Pope Francis summarizes what he means by dialogue: "Approaching, speaking, listening, looking at, coming to know and understand one another, and to find common ground: all these things are summed up in the one word 'dialogue'" (no. 198). This is all the more necessary when we look at the rise in conflicts of all sorts in all parts of the world. The aim of such a dialogical model of government and society is to promote kindness and a "culture of encounter," which sets up well the final two chapters of *Fratelli Tutti*.[15]

Chapter seven introduces an important but not as often discussed theme among Christians in the world today: reconciliation. Pope Francis is keen to note that social change cannot simply take place as if history does not exist and the past did not happen. While forgiveness is essential in the Christian life, we are not meant to merely "forgive and forget," but rather to remember the victims and survivors of violence and injustice. In this section of the encyclical the pope also reiterates the inadmissibility of the death penalty and the need to reject war.

In chapter eight the pope, again living up to his namesake's legacy, reminds us of both the importance of interreligious dialogue and the more fundamental identity we have as humans who are part of one divine family. Religion, therefore, should serve this sense of universal human *fraternitas*. I am reminded in this closing section of *Fratelli Tutti* of one of the last talks that the Trappist monk and author Thomas Merton gave before his untimely death in 1968. Speaking to a group of Christian monks in Asia, Merton said that prior to dialogue and communication there is a deeper level of connection that we Christians call *communion*. He adds: "It is wordless. It is beyond words, and it is beyond speech, and it is beyond concept. Not that we discover a new unity. We discover an older unity. My dear brothers, we are already one. But we imagine that we are not. And what we have to recover is our original unity. What we

---

[15] For more on the Catholic notion of encounter, see Marcus Mescher, *The Ethics of Encounter: Christian Neighbor Love as a Practice of Solidarity* (Maryknoll, NY: Orbis Books, 2020).

have to be is what we are."[16] Truly, this sense of communion about which Merton speaks so eloquently illustrates well the concept of *fraternitas* that Pope Francis wishes to present to the church and world.

Situating *Fratelli Tutti* within the History of Catholic Social Teaching

Despite what some naysayers and enthusiasts alike might wish to believe, *Fratelli Tutti* is not cut out of whole cloth as if it were some entirely novel teaching by some extremely innovative pontiff. Like its predecessor encyclical *Laudato Si'*, this document builds on the previous magisterial documents promulgated over the course of the last century. This tradition of authoritative instruction is known as Catholic social teaching.[17] As with each contribution made over the years by a host of popes including Leo XIII, Pius XI, John XXIII, Paul VI, John Paul II, and Benedict XVI, Pope Francis's latest addition to the tradition draws from the important work of his predecessors while adding some clarifications and developments. The pope summarizes the aim and scope of the encyclical in the opening:

> The following pages do not claim to offer a complete teaching on fraternal love, but rather to consider its universal scope, its openness to every man and woman. I offer this social Encyclical as a modest contribution to continued reflection, in the hope that in the face of present-day attempts to eliminate and ignore others, we may prove capable of responding with a new vision of fraternity and social friendship that will not remain at the level of words. (no. 6)

---

[16] Thomas Merton, *The Asian Journal of Thomas Merton*, ed. Naomi Burton, Patrick Hart, and James Laughlin (New York: New Directions, 1973), 308.

[17] For a succinct and insightful introduction, see Edward P. DeBerri et al., *Catholic Social Teaching: Our Best Kept Secret*, 4th ed. (Maryknoll, NY: Orbis Books, 2003).

There are a number of key principles that form the focal point and structure of Catholic social teaching. Over the years there have been different efforts to summarize the central elements. In 1998 the United States Conference of Catholic Bishops (USCCB) issued a document titled "Sharing Catholic Social Teaching: Challenges and Directions," which outlined seven major themes of Catholic social teaching.[18] These key principles include: (1) the dignity of the human person; (2) the human person in community; (3) the dignity of work and rights of workers; (4) option for the poor and vulnerable; (5) solidarity; (6) care for creation; and (7) rights and responsibilities. *Fratelli Tutti* touches on all seven key principles, referencing the magisterial documents of the pope's predecessors while also drawing wisdom from a variety of other sources, especially regional conferences of Catholic bishops throughout the world. This last point is something distinctive about Pope Francis's contribution in his writings; he is always emphasizing the interrelationship between global concerns and the insights of local churches responding to those concerns around the world.

There are numerous resources already available that provide excellent introductions to and analysis of the century-old Catholic tradition of social teaching.[19] For that reason, I want only to point out a few examples here of *Fratelli Tutti's* continuity with and dependence on previous documents in the church's social teaching. Among the most important themes that appear continually throughout the encyclical is that of the universal and inalienable dignity of the human person. In Paul VI's 1967 encyclical *Populorum Progressio* we are reminded that "human

---

[18] See USCCB, "Sharing Catholic Social Teaching: Challenges and Directions," June 19, 1998.

[19] For example, see David J. O'Brien and Thomas A. Shannon, eds., *Catholic Social Thought: The Documentary Heritage*, expanded ed. (Maryknoll, NY: Orbis Books, 2010); Charles E. Curran, *Catholic Social Teaching: A Historical, Theological, and Ethical Analysis* (Washington, DC: Georgetown University Press, 2002); and Kenneth R. Himes, ed., *Modern Catholic Social Teaching: Commentaries and Interpretations* (Washington, DC: Georgetown University Press, 2005).

dignity is the result of human existence. It is not earned by achievements or bestowed by any authorities other than God."[20] This is also a recurring theme in *Fratelli Tutti,* as Pope Francis critiques the current social and global circumstances that often reduce people's dignity to an evaluation of their material wealth or demonstrable contributions. John Paul II, in his 1987 encyclical *Sollicitudo Rei Socialis,* also emphasizes this point, noting the ways that economic inequality and poverty diminish the inherent dignity and value of human personhood established by God. Pope Francis cites both of these texts and develops these same themes for our contemporary context.

Likewise, the theme of the common good appears regularly throughout *Fratelli Tutti.* Recognized as the essential goal and purpose of human government, promotion and protection of the common good is something that Catholic social teaching recognizes as flowing from our human vocation as persons in community. Pope Francis draws from *Sollicitudo Rei Socialis* again, as well as John Paul II's 1991 encyclical *Centesimus Annus,* at various points throughout *Fratelli Tutti* to reiterate the centrality of the common good and the importance of work in protecting and maintaining human dignity.

Perhaps the most recognizable principle of Catholic social teaching is that of solidarity, which appears in *Fratelli Tutti* more than twenty-five times. Here Pope Francis builds on the work of John XXIII, Paul VI, John Paul II, and Benedict XVI in emphasizing the interrelatedness of the human family and the importance of our acknowledgment of interdependence. For Pope Francis, solidarity is not merely a theme for the human family alone, but is also something that we are called to recognize in terms of "integral ecology," as he describes it in his 2015 encyclical *Laudato Si'.* There is an intrinsic relationship humanity has to nonhuman creation, which also calls for greater reflection, discernment, and action on behalf of justice.

---

[20] Paul VI, *Populorum Progressio* (1967), as summarized in DeBerri, *Catholic Social Teaching,* 20.

To be clear, Pope Francis is not merely repeating what has come before him, as inspirational and important as those teachings are. The pope is also *building* on to the tradition of Catholic social teaching, and he does so in at least three notable ways. The first is a clarification about the inadmissibility of the death penalty. Pointing to earlier magisterial teaching that sets the stage, notably John Paul II's 1995 encyclical *Evangelium Vitae*, Pope Francis emphasizes that "Saint John Paul II stated clearly and firmly that the death penalty is inadequate from a moral standpoint and no longer necessary from that of penal justice. There can be no stepping back from this position. Today we state clearly that 'the death penalty is inadmissible' and the Church is firmly committed to calling for its abolition world-wide" (no. 263). The pope also cites the 2018 revision of the *Catechism of the Catholic Church,* in which the inadmissibility of the death penalty is articulated directly.[21]

The second is a contribution to a millennia-old discussion in the church that dates back to at least Saint Augustine of Hippo (d. 430 CE); that is, what criteria—if any—we can use to evaluate whether war is justified. This topic is less clearly decided in *Fratelli Tutti* than the closed case of the death penalty. When it comes to what is known as the just-war theory, Pope Francis takes a hard look at the realities of our world in these modern times, noting the dire truth that "conditions that favour the outbreak of wars are once again increasing" and, therefore, "if we want true integral human development for all, we must work tirelessly to avoid war between nations and peoples" (no. 257). In response, the pope explains in paragraph 258 that there have been too many false excuses issued by nations and peoples to justify their violent actions and the launchings of wars. Citing the *Catechism*'s acknowledgment of the church's longstanding just-war criteria, Pope Francis expresses serious

---

[21] See Congregation for the Doctrine of the Faith, "Letter to the Bishops regarding the Revision of No. 2267 of the Catechism of the Catholic Church on the Death Penalty," August 1, 2018.

doubt about whether such conditions could ever be met in an age marked by weapons entirely inconceivable to the great Christian thinkers—like Saint Augustine and Saint Thomas Aquinas (d. 1274)—who have contributed to the development of just-war theory over the centuries. Pope Francis explains:

> At issue is whether the development of nuclear, chemical and biological weapons, and the enormous and growing possibilities offered by new technologies, have granted war an uncontrollable destructive power over great numbers of innocent civilians. The truth is that "never has humanity had such power over itself, yet nothing ensures that it will be used wisely." We can no longer think of war as a solution, because its risks will probably always be greater than its supposed benefits. In view of this, it is very difficult nowadays to invoke the rational criteria elaborated in earlier centuries to speak of the possibility of a "just war." Never again war! (no. 258)

While coming just shy of definitively precluding any possibility of a "just" war, the pope signals to theological ethicists, pastoral ministers, and world leaders alike that this remains a pressing and important question.

Finally, while not new for Pope Francis, as demonstrated in his other writings and addresses, the citation of non-Christian sources remains a significant and inspirational inclusion in *Fratelli Tutti*. In particular, the pope opens and closes the encyclical with reference to the encounter he had with Grand Imam Ahmad Al-Tayyeb in 2019, which resulted in a joint statement on human solidarity and fraternity. Near the very end of *Fratelli Tutti* Pope Francis cites a long passage from this joint statement (no. 285) and makes reference to it eight other times in the encyclical. He also cites Rabbi Hillel (nos. 59–60), thereby acknowledging insights from leaders of the other Abrahamic religions of Judaism and Islam. The continued emphasis on dialogue, especially within an interreligious context, is a hallmark of Pope Francis's ministry and outreach, which offers the church an opportunity to build on the foundational work of the Second Vatican Council, especially its 1965 *Decree on Non-Christian Religions (Nostra Aetate)*. When it comes to promoting *fraternitas* throughout the whole human family, it cannot be left to Christians alone, but to those of all faith traditions—and no faith tradition at all—to join together in solidarity to work for peace, justice, and the integrity of creation.

The Absence of Women in the Text

Before leaving you to explore the document itself, it is important to note one major issue with *Fratelli Tutti* that has rightly garnered much attention, namely, the absence of women. While Pope Francis does regularly invoke the inclusive phrases "men and women" and "brothers and sisters" throughout the encyclical, it is striking that *no women are cited* in the text. This is jarring and, frankly, disappointing. Prior to the encyclical's release, as discussed above, there was a lot of consternation about the odd titular choice in naming this encyclical *Fratelli Tutti,* an Italian translation of the original Latin phrase (*omnes fratres*) used by Saint Francis when addressing an *entirely male audience* in the 1220s. This is not a critique of Saint Francis, for it would have been very odd in the thirteenth century to use a gender-inclusive address in a setting that included only male Franciscan friars. But there is no clear justification for maintaining the gender exclusivity in a modern language (Italian) in the contemporary context (the year 2020). To many, this was not at all surprising, yet to me it remains a gratuitous oversight that is not really justifiable.

More startling, though, is the absence of women as theological sources or models of Christian discipleship in the text itself. As theologian Meghan Clark notes,

> At the very end, despite the pope saying he's been inspired by "brothers and sisters," it is only three men Francis lists: Martin Luther King Jr., Desmond Tutu, and Mahatma Gandhi. This is particularly striking because

much of the local community-building work called for by this encyclical is practiced and embodied by women, especially within the contexts of migration and post-conflict reconciliation.[22]

Indeed, some of the most visible, inspirational, and powerful models of peacemaking, reconciliation, and solidarity have been women. I think of the 2011 Nobel Peace Prize recipients Ellen Johnson Sirleaf and Leymah Gbowee of Liberia and Tawakkol Karman of Yemen for their extraordinary contributions to peacemaking efforts.[23] Or, Malala Yousafzai of Pakistan, who shared the 2014 Nobel Peace Prize for her contributions in the "struggle against the suppression of children and young people and for the right of all children to education."[24] Yousafzai was shot in the face by the Taliban for her activism on behalf of the rights of girls and women to receive an education. Or, perhaps Pope Francis could have again cited Dorothy Day, the co-founder of the Catholic Worker Movement, whom he mentioned as a model for Christian discipleship in his 2015 address to the United States Congress.[25] The list could easily continue.

This last part of my introduction is not intended to sour one's reading of the important encyclical *Fratelli Tutti,* nor do I wish to minimize in any way the profound significance of its content. However, it must be stated that the stark absence of women's voices and female examples cannot be overlooked. *Fratelli Tutti* is indeed a landmark contribution to Catholic social teaching, one that will certainly inspire and challenge men *and women* in living the Christian life more authentically for generations. But the journey toward full inclusivity remains as great a challenge for the church as it does for other communities and nations

---

[22] Meghan Clark, "'Fratelli Tutti' Shares Practical Wisdom, But Lacks Insights of Women," *National Catholic Reporter,* October 5, 2020.

[23] See "The Nobel Peace Prize for 2011," https://www.nobelprize.org.

[24] See "The Nobel Peace Prize for 2014," https://www.nobelprize.org.

[25] See Pope Francis, "Address of the Holy Father: Visit to the Joint Session of the United States Congress," September 24, 2015.

around the world. Perhaps it is fitting to close this section with reference to an important passage in the encyclical, which appears without irony, yet remains a challenge to Pope Francis himself and the broader church community: "The organization of societies worldwide is still far from reflecting clearly that women possess the same dignity and identical rights as men. We say one thing with words, but our decisions and reality tell another story" (no. 23).

Conclusion

Pope Francis and his ability to embody many of the core principles of his medieval namesake, Saint Francis of Assisi, continually impress me as a Franciscan friar and theologian. *Fratelli Tutti*, while certainly an imperfect document, nevertheless reflects some of the most important elements of the Franciscan vision of social, ecclesial, and world relationships, all of which ought to begin with the centrality of relationship and the prioritization of the needs of those most vulnerable in our communities. The way this is made manifest in each new time and place is through embracing the distinctively Franciscan principle of *fraternitas*, recognizing that we are always already connected to one another as sisters and brothers, children of the same God who calls us to be reflections of divine mercy, justice, and peace. In a historic moment when both local and global contexts are defined by tremendous division and sectarian polarization, *Fratelli Tutti* offers the church and world a sign of hope and an invitation for readers to become instruments of God's peace.

ENCYCLICAL LETTER
FRATELLI TUTTI
OF THE HOLY FATHER
FRANCIS
ON FRATERNITY AND SOCIAL FRIENDSHIP

1. *"FRATELLI TUTTI."*[1] With these words, Saint Francis of
Assisi addressed his brothers and sisters and proposed to them
a way of life marked by the flavour of the Gospel. Of the coun-
sels Francis offered, I would like to select the one in which he
calls for a love that transcends the barriers of geography and
distance, and declares blessed all those who love their brother
"as much when he is far away from him as when he is with
him."[2] In his simple and direct way, Saint Francis expressed the
essence of a fraternal openness that allows us to acknowledge,
appreciate and love each person, regardless of physical proxim-
ity, regardless of where he or she was born or lives.

---

[1] *Admonitions*, 6, 1. English translation in *Francis of Assisi: Early Documents*, vol 1., New York, London, Manila (1999), 131.

[2] Ibid., 25: op. cit., 136.

2. This saint of fraternal love, simplicity and joy, who inspired me to write the Encyclical *Laudato Si'*, prompts me once more to devote this new Encyclical to fraternity and social friendship. Francis felt himself a brother to the sun, the sea and the wind, yet he knew that he was even closer to those of his own flesh. Wherever he went, he sowed seeds of peace and walked alongside the poor, the abandoned, the infirm and the outcast, the least of his brothers and sisters.

WITHOUT BORDERS

3. There is an episode in the life of Saint Francis that shows his openness of heart, which knew no bounds and transcended differences of origin, nationality, colour or religion. It was his visit to Sultan Malik-el-Kamil, in Egypt, which entailed considerable hardship, given Francis' poverty, his scarce resources, the great distances to be traveled and their differences of language, culture and religion. That journey, undertaken at the time of the Crusades, further demonstrated the breadth and grandeur of his love, which sought to embrace everyone. Francis' fidelity to his Lord was commensurate with his love for his brothers and sisters. Unconcerned for the hardships and dangers involved, Francis went to meet the Sultan with the same attitude that he instilled in his disciples: if they found themselves "among the Saracens and other nonbelievers," without renouncing their own identity they were not to "engage in arguments or disputes, but to be subject to every human creature for God's sake."[3] In the context of the times, this was an extraordinary recommendation. We are impressed that some eight hundred years ago Saint Francis urged that all forms of hostility or conflict be avoided and that a humble and fraternal "subjection" be shown to those who did not share his faith.

---

[3] SAINT FRANCIS OF ASSISI, *Earlier Rule of the Friars Minor (Regula non bullata)*, 16: 3.6: op. cit. 74.

4. Francis did not wage a war of words aimed at imposing doctrines; he simply spread the love of God. He understood that "God is love and those who abide in love abide in God" (*1 Jn* 4:16). In this way, he became a father to all and inspired the vision of a fraternal society. Indeed, "only the man who approaches others, not to draw them into his own life, but to help them become ever more fully themselves, can truly be called a father."[4] In the world of that time, bristling with watchtowers and defensive walls, cities were a theatre of brutal wars between powerful families, even as poverty was spreading through the countryside. Yet there Francis was able to welcome true peace into his heart and free himself of the desire to wield power over others. He became one of the poor and sought to live in harmony with all. Francis has inspired these pages.

5. Issues of human fraternity and social friendship have always been a concern of mine. In recent years, I have spoken of them repeatedly and in different settings. In this Encyclical, I have sought to bring together many of those statements and to situate them in a broader context of reflection. In the preparation of *Laudato Si'*, I had a source of inspiration in my brother Bartholomew, the Orthodox Patriarch, who has spoken forcefully of our need to care for creation. In this case, I have felt particularly encouraged by the Grand Imam Ahmad Al-Tayyeb, with whom I met in Abu Dhabi, where we declared that "God has created all human beings equal in rights, duties and dignity, and has called them to live together as brothers and sisters."[5] This was no mere diplomatic gesture, but a reflection born of dialogue and common commitment. The present Encyclical takes up and develops some of the great themes raised in the Document that we both signed. I have also incorporated,

---

[4] ELOI LECLERC, O.F.M., *Exil et tendresse*, Éd. Franciscaines, Paris, 1962, 205.

[5] *Document on Human Fraternity for World Peace and Living Together*, Abu Dhabi (4 February 2019): *L'Osservatore Romano*, 4-5 February 2019, p. 6.

along with my own thoughts, a number of letters, documents and considerations that I have received from many individuals and groups throughout the world.

6. The following pages do not claim to offer a complete teaching on fraternal love, but rather to consider its universal scope, its openness to every man and woman. I offer this social Encyclical as a modest contribution to continued reflection, in the hope that in the face of present-day attempts to eliminate or ignore others, we may prove capable of responding with a new vision of fraternity and social friendship that will not remain at the level of words. Although I have written it from the Christian convictions that inspire and sustain me, I have sought to make this reflection an invitation to dialogue among all people of good will.

7. As I was writing this letter, the Covid-19 pandemic unexpectedly erupted, exposing our false securities. Aside from the different ways that various countries responded to the crisis, their inability to work together became quite evident. For all our hyper-connectivity, we witnessed a fragmentation that made it more difficult to resolve problems that affect us all. Anyone who thinks that the only lesson to be learned was the need to improve what we were already doing, or to refine existing systems and regulations, is denying reality.

8. It is my desire that, in this our time, by acknowledging the dignity of each human person, we can contribute to the rebirth of a universal aspiration to fraternity. Fraternity between all men and women. "Here we have a splendid secret that shows us how to dream and to turn our life into a wonderful adventure. No one can face life in isolation… We need a community that supports and helps us, in which we can help one another to keep looking ahead. How important it is to dream together… By ourselves, we risk seeing mirages, things that are not there.

Dreams, on the other hand, are built together."[6] Let us dream, then, as a single human family, as fellow travelers sharing the same flesh, as children of the same earth which is our common home, each of us bringing the richness of his or her beliefs and convictions, each of us with his or her own voice, brothers and sisters all.

CHAPTER ONE

DARK CLOUDS OVER A CLOSED WORLD

9. Without claiming to carry out an exhaustive analysis or to study every aspect of our present-day experience, I intend simply to consider certain trends in our world that hinder the development of universal fraternity.

SHATTERED DREAMS

10. For decades, it seemed that the world had learned a lesson from its many wars and disasters, and was slowly moving towards various forms of integration. For example, there was the dream of a united Europe, capable of acknowledging its shared roots and rejoicing in its rich diversity. We think of "the firm conviction of the founders of the European Union, who envisioned a future based on the capacity to work together in bridging divisions and in fostering peace and fellowship between all the peoples of this continent."[7] There was also a growing desire for integration in Latin America, and several steps were taken in this direction. In some countries and regions, attempts at

---

[6] *Address at the Ecumenical and Interreligious Meeting with Young People*, Skopje, North Macedonia (7 May 2019): *L'Osservatore Romano*, 9 May 2019, p. 9.

[7] *Address to the European Parliament*, Strasbourg (25 November 2014): AAS 106 (2014), 996.

reconciliation and rapprochement proved fruitful, while others showed great promise.

11. Our own days, however, seem to be showing signs of a certain regression. Ancient conflicts thought long buried are breaking out anew, while instances of a myopic, extremist, resentful and aggressive nationalism are on the rise. In some countries, a concept of popular and national unity influenced by various ideologies is creating new forms of selfishness and a loss of the social sense under the guise of defending national interests. Once more we are being reminded that "each new generation must take up the struggles and attainments of past generations, while setting its sights even higher. This is the path. Goodness, together with love, justice and solidarity, are not achieved once and for all; they have to be realized each day. It is not possible to settle for what was achieved in the past and complacently enjoy it, as if we could somehow disregard the fact that many of our brothers and sisters still endure situations that cry out for our attention."[8]

12. "Opening up to the world" is an expression that has been co-opted by the economic and financial sector and is now used exclusively of openness to foreign interests or to the freedom of economic powers to invest without obstacles or complications in all countries. Local conflicts and disregard for the common good are exploited by the global economy in order to impose a single cultural model. This culture unifies the world, but divides persons and nations, for "as society becomes ever more globalized, it makes us neighbours, but does not make us brothers."[9] We are more alone than ever in an increasingly massified world that promotes individual interests and weakens the communitarian dimension of life. Indeed, there are markets

---

[8] *Meeting with Authorities, Civil Society and the Diplomatic Corps*, Santiago, Chile (16 January 2018): AAS 110 (2018), 256.

[9] BENEDICT XVI, Encyclical Letter *Caritas in Veritate* (29 June 2009), 19: AAS 101 (2009), 655.

where individuals become mere consumers or bystanders. As a rule, the advance of this kind of globalism strengthens the identity of the more powerful, who can protect themselves, but it tends to diminish the identity of the weaker and poorer regions, making them more vulnerable and dependent. In this way, political life becomes increasingly fragile in the face of transnational economic powers that operate with the principle of "divide and conquer."

The end of historical consciousness

13. As a result, there is a growing loss of the sense of history, which leads to even further breakup. A kind of "deconstructionism," whereby human freedom claims to create everything starting from zero, is making headway in today's culture. The one thing it leaves in its wake is the drive to limitless consumption and expressions of empty individualism. Concern about this led me to offer the young some advice. "If someone tells young people to ignore their history, to reject the experiences of their elders, to look down on the past and to look forward to a future that he himself holds out, doesn't it then become easy to draw them along so that they only do what he tells them? He needs the young to be shallow, uprooted and distrustful, so that they can trust only in his promises and act according to his plans. That is how various ideologies operate: they destroy (or deconstruct) all differences so that they can reign unopposed. To do so, however, they need young people who have no use for history, who spurn the spiritual and human riches inherited from past generations, and are ignorant of everything that came before them."[10]

14. These are the new forms of cultural colonization. Let us not forget that "peoples that abandon their tradition and, either from a craze to mimic others or to foment violence, or from

---

[10] Post-Synodal Apostolic Exhortation *Christus vivit* (25 March 2019), 181.

unpardonable negligence or apathy, allow others to rob their very soul, end up losing not only their spiritual identity but also their moral consistency and, in the end, their intellectual, economic and political independence."[11] One effective way to weaken historical consciousness, critical thinking, the struggle for justice and the processes of integration is to empty great words of their meaning or to manipulate them. Nowadays, what do certain words like democracy, freedom, justice or unity really mean? They have been bent and shaped to serve as tools for domination, as meaningless tags that can be used to justify any action.

LACKING A PLAN FOR EVERYONE

15. The best way to dominate and gain control over people is to spread despair and discouragement, even under the guise of defending certain values. Today, in many countries, hyperbole, extremism and polarization have become political tools. Employing a strategy of ridicule, suspicion and relentless criticism, in a variety of ways one denies the right of others to exist or to have an opinion. Their share of the truth and their values are rejected and, as a result, the life of society is impoverished and subjected to the hubris of the powerful. Political life no longer has to do with healthy debates about long-term plans to improve people's lives and to advance the common good, but only with slick marketing techniques primarily aimed at discrediting others. In this craven exchange of charges and counter-charges, debate degenerates into a permanent state of disagreement and confrontation.

16. Amid the fray of conflicting interests, where victory consists in eliminating one's opponents, how is it possible to raise our sights to recognize our neighbours or to help those who have

---

[11] CARDINAL RAÚL SILVA HENRÍQUEZ, *Homily at the Te Deum*, Santiago de Chile (18 September 1974).

fallen along the way? A plan that would set great goals for the development of our entire human family nowadays sounds like madness. We are growing ever more distant from one another, while the slow and demanding march towards an increasingly united and just world is suffering a new and dramatic setback.

17. To care for the world in which we live means to care for ourselves. Yet we need to think of ourselves more and more as a single family dwelling in a common home. Such care does not interest those economic powers that demand quick profits. Often the voices raised in defence of the environment are silenced or ridiculed, using apparently reasonable arguments that are merely a screen for special interests. In this shallow, short-sighted culture that we have created, bereft of a shared vision, "it is foreseeable that, once certain resources have been depleted, the scene will be set for new wars, albeit under the guise of noble claims."[12]

A "throwaway" world

18. Some parts of our human family, it appears, can be readily sacrificed for the sake of others considered worthy of a carefree existence. Ultimately, "persons are no longer seen as a paramount value to be cared for and respected, especially when they are poor and disabled, 'not yet useful' – like the unborn, or 'no longer needed' – like the elderly. We have grown indifferent to all kinds of wastefulness, starting with the waste of food, which is deplorable in the extreme."[13]

19. A decline in the birthrate, which leads to the aging of the population, together with the relegation of the elderly to a sad and lonely existence, is a subtle way of stating that it is all about

---

[12] Encyclical Letter *Laudato Si'* (24 May 2015), 57: AAS 107 (2015), 869.

[13] *Address to the Diplomatic Corps accredited to the Holy See* (11 January 2016): AAS 108 (2016), 120.

us, that our individual concerns are the only thing that matters. In this way, "what is thrown away are not only food and dispensable objects, but often human beings themselves."[14] We have seen what happened with the elderly in certain places in our world as a result of the coronavirus. They did not have to die that way. Yet something similar had long been occurring during heat waves and in other situations: older people found themselves cruelly abandoned. We fail to realize that, by isolating the elderly and leaving them in the care of others without the closeness and concern of family members, we disfigure and impoverish the family itself. We also end up depriving young people of a necessary connection to their roots and a wisdom that the young cannot achieve on their own.

20. This way of discarding others can take a variety of forms, such as an obsession with reducing labour costs with no concern for its grave consequences, since the unemployment that it directly generates leads to the expansion of poverty.[15] In addition, a readiness to discard others finds expression in vicious attitudes that we thought long past, such as racism, which retreats underground only to keep reemerging. Instances of racism continue to shame us, for they show that our supposed social progress is not as real or definitive as we think.

21. Some economic rules have proved effective for growth, but not for integral human development.[16] Wealth has increased, but together with inequality, with the result that "new forms of poverty are emerging."[17] The claim that the modern world has reduced poverty is made by measuring poverty with criteria

---

[14] *Address to the Diplomatic Corps accredited to the Holy See* (13 January 2014): AAS 106 (2014), 83-84.

[15] Cf. *Address to the "Centesimus Annus pro Pontifice" Foundation* (25 May 2013): *Insegnamenti* I, 1 (2013), 238.

[16] Cf. SAINT PAUL VI, Encyclical Letter *Populorum Progressio* (26 March 1967): AAS 59 (1967), 264.

[17] BENEDICT XVI, Encyclical Letter *Caritas in Veritate* (29 June 2009), 22: AAS 101 (2009), 657.

from the past that do not correspond to present-day realities. In other times, for example, lack of access to electric energy was not considered a sign of poverty, nor was it a source of hardship. Poverty must always be understood and gauged in the context of the actual opportunities available in each concrete historical period.

Insufficiently universal human rights

22. It frequently becomes clear that, in practice, human rights are not equal for all. Respect for those rights "is the preliminary condition for a country's social and economic development. When the dignity of the human person is respected, and his or her rights recognized and guaranteed, creativity and interdependence thrive, and the creativity of the human personality is released through actions that further the common good."[18] Yet, "by closely observing our contemporary societies, we see numerous contradictions that lead us to wonder whether the equal dignity of all human beings, solemnly proclaimed seventy years ago, is truly recognized, respected, protected and promoted in every situation. In today's world, many forms of injustice persist, fed by reductive anthropological visions and by a profit-based economic model that does not hesitate to exploit, discard and even kill human beings. While one part of humanity lives in opulence, another part sees its own dignity denied, scorned or trampled upon, and its fundamental rights discarded or violated."[19] What does this tell us about the equality of rights grounded in innate human dignity?

23. Similarly, the organization of societies worldwide is still far from reflecting clearly that women possess the same dignity

---

[18] *Address to the Civil Authorities*, Tirana, Albania (21 September 2014): AAS 106 (2014), 773.

[19] *Message to Participants in the International Conference "Human Rights in the Contemporary World: Achievements, Omissions, Negations"* (10 December 2018): *L'Osservatore Romano*, 10-11 December 2018, p. 8.

and identical rights as men. We say one thing with words, but our decisions and reality tell another story. Indeed, "doubly poor are those women who endure situations of exclusion, mistreatment and violence, since they are frequently less able to defend their rights."[20]

24. We should also recognize that "even though the international community has adopted numerous agreements aimed at ending slavery in all its forms, and has launched various strategies to combat this phenomenon, millions of people today – children, women and men of all ages – are deprived of freedom and forced to live in conditions akin to slavery… Today, as in the past, slavery is rooted in a notion of the human person that allows him or her to be treated as an object… Whether by coercion, or deception, or by physical or psychological duress, human persons created in the image and likeness of God are deprived of their freedom, sold and reduced to being the property of others. They are treated as means to an end… are skilled in using modern means of communication as a way of luring young men and women in various parts of the world."[21] A perversion that exceeds all limits when it subjugates women and then forces them to abort. An abomination that goes to the length of kidnapping persons for the sake of selling their organs. Trafficking in persons and other contemporary forms of enslavement are a worldwide problem that needs to be taken seriously by humanity as a whole: "since criminal organizations employ global networks to achieve their goals, efforts to eliminate this phenomenon also demand a common and, indeed, a global effort on the part of various sectors of society."[22]

---

[20] Apostolic Exhortation *Evangelii Gaudium* (24 November 2013), 212: AAS 105 (2013), 1108

[21] *Message for the 2015 World Day of Peace* (8 December 2014), 3-4: AAS 107 (2015), 69-71.

[22] *Ibid.*, 5: AAS 107 (2015), 72.

Conflict and fear

25. War, terrorist attacks, racial or religious persecution, and many other affronts to human dignity are judged differently, depending on how convenient it proves for certain, primarily economic, interests. What is true as long as it is convenient for someone in power stops being true once it becomes inconvenient. These situations of violence, sad to say, "have become so common as to constitute a real 'third world war' fought piecemeal."[23]

26. This should not be surprising, if we realize that we no longer have common horizons that unite us; indeed, the first victim of every war is "the human family's innate vocation to fraternity." As a result, "every threatening situation breeds mistrust and leads people to withdraw into their own safety zone."[24] Our world is trapped in a strange contradiction: we believe that we can "ensure stability and peace through a false sense of security sustained by a mentality of fear and mistrust."[25]

27. Paradoxically, we have certain ancestral fears that technological development has not succeeded in eliminating; indeed, those fears have been able to hide and spread behind new technologies. Today too, outside the ancient town walls lies the abyss, the territory of the unknown, the wilderness. Whatever comes from there cannot be trusted, for it is unknown, unfamiliar, not part of the village. It is the territory of the "barbarian," from whom we must defend ourselves at all costs. As a result, new walls are erected for self-preservation, the outside

---

[23] *Message for the 2016 World Day of Peace* (8 December 2015), 2: AAS 108 (2016), 49.

[24] *Message fro the 2020 World Day of Peace* (8 December 2019), 1: *L'Osservatore Romano*, 13 December 2019, p. 8.

[25] *Address on Nuclear Weapons*, Nagasaki, Japan (24 November 2019): *L'Osservatore Romano*, 25-26 November 2019, p. 6.

world ceases to exist and leaves only "my" world, to the point that others, no longer considered human beings possessed of an inalienable dignity, become only "them." Once more, we encounter "the temptation to build a culture of walls, to raise walls, walls in the heart, walls on the land, in order to prevent this encounter with other cultures, with other people. And those who raise walls will end up as slaves within the very walls they have built. They are left without horizons, for they lack this interchange with others."[26]

28. The loneliness, fear and insecurity experienced by those who feel abandoned by the system creates a fertile terrain for various "mafias." These flourish because they claim to be defenders of the forgotten, often by providing various forms of assistance even as they pursue their criminal interests. There also exists a typically "mafioso" pedagogy that, by appealing to a false communitarian mystique, creates bonds of dependency and fealty from which it is very difficult to break free.

GLOBALIZATION AND PROGRESS WITHOUT A SHARED ROADMAP

29. With the Grand Imam Ahmad Al-Tayyeb, we do not ignore the positive advances made in the areas of science, technology, medicine, industry and welfare, above all in developed countries. Nonetheless, "we wish to emphasize that, together with these historical advances, great and valued as they are, there exists a moral deterioration that influences international action and a weakening of spiritual values and responsibility. This contributes to a general feeling of frustration, isolation and desperation." We see "outbreaks of tension and a buildup of arms and ammunition in a global context dominated by uncertainty, disillusionment, fear of the future, and controlled by narrow economic interests." We can also point to "major

---

[26] *Dialogue with Students and Teachers of the San Carlo College in Milan* (6 April 2019): *L'Osservatore Romano*, 8-9 April 2019, p. 6.

political crises, situations of injustice and the lack of an equitable distribution of natural resources... In the face of such crises that result in the deaths of millions of children – emaciated from poverty and hunger – there is an unacceptable silence on the international level."[27] This panorama, for all its undeniable advances, does not appear to lead to a more humane future.

30. In today's world, the sense of belonging to a single human family is fading, and the dream of working together for justice and peace seems an outdated utopia. What reigns instead is a cool, comfortable and globalized indifference, born of deep disillusionment concealed behind a deceptive illusion: thinking that we are all-powerful, while failing to realize that we are all in the same boat. This illusion, unmindful of the great fraternal values, leads to "a sort of cynicism. For that is the temptation we face if we go down the road of disenchantment and disappointment... Isolation and withdrawal into one's own interests are never the way to restore hope and bring about renewal. Rather, it is closeness; it is the culture of encounter. Isolation, no; closeness, yes. Culture clash, no; culture of encounter, yes."[28]

31. In this world that races ahead, yet lacks a shared roadmap, we increasingly sense that "the gap between concern for one's personal well-being and the prosperity of the larger human family seems to be stretching to the point of complete division between individuals and human community... It is one thing to feel forced to live together, but something entirely different to value the richness and beauty of those seeds of common life that need to be sought out and cultivated."[29] Technology is

---

[27] *Document on Human Fraternity for World Peace and Living Together*, Abu Dhabi (4 February 2019): *L'Osservatore Romano*, 4-5 February 2019, p. 6.

[28] *Address to the World of Culture, Cagliari, Italy* (22 September 2013): *L'Osservatore Romano*, 23-24 September 2013, p. 7.

[29] *Humana Communitas. Letter to the President of the Pontifical Academy for Life on the Twenty-fifth Anniversary of its Founding* (6 January 2019),

constantly advancing, yet "how wonderful it would be if the growth of scientific and technological innovation could come with more equality and social inclusion. How wonderful would it be, even as we discover faraway planets, to rediscover the needs of the brothers and sisters who orbit around us."[30]

PANDEMICS AND OTHER CALAMITIES IN HISTORY

32. True, a worldwide tragedy like the Covid-19 pandemic momentarily revived the sense that we are a global community, all in the same boat, where one person's problems are the problems of all. Once more we realized that no one is saved alone; we can only be saved together. As I said in those days, "the storm has exposed our vulnerability and uncovered those false and superfluous certainties around which we constructed our daily schedules, our projects, our habits and priorities... Amid this storm, the façade of those stereotypes with which we camouflaged our egos, always worrying about appearances, has fallen away, revealing once more the ineluctable and blessed awareness that we are part of one another, that we are brothers and sisters of one another."[31]

33. The world was relentlessly moving towards an economy that, thanks to technological progress, sought to reduce "human costs"; there were those who would have had us believe that freedom of the market was sufficient to keep everything secure. Yet the brutal and unforeseen blow of this uncontrolled pandemic forced us to recover our concern for human beings, for everyone, rather than for the benefit of a few. Today we can recognize that "we fed ourselves on dreams of splendour and grandeur, and ended up consuming distraction, insularity and

---

2.6: *L'Osservatore Romano*, 16 January 2019, pp. 6-7.

[30] *Video Message to the TED Conference in Vancouver* (26 April 2017): *L'Osservatore Romano*, 27 April 2017, p. 7.

[31] *Extraordinary Moment of Prayer in Time of Epidemic* (27 March 2020): *L'Osservatore Romano*, 29 March 2020, p. 10.

solitude. We gorged ourselves on networking, and lost the taste of fraternity. We looked for quick and safe results, only to find ourselves overwhelmed by impatience and anxiety. Prisoners of a virtual reality, we lost the taste and flavour of the truly real."[32] The pain, uncertainty and fear, and the realization of our own limitations, brought on by the pandemic have only made it all the more urgent that we rethink our styles of life, our relationships, the organization of our societies and, above all, the meaning of our existence.

34. If everything is connected, it is hard to imagine that this global disaster is unrelated to our way of approaching reality, our claim to be absolute masters of our own lives and of all that exists. I do not want to speak of divine retribution, nor would it be sufficient to say that the harm we do to nature is itself the punishment for our offences. The world is itself crying out in rebellion. We are reminded of the well-known verse of the poet Virgil that evokes the "tears of things," the misfortunes of life and history.[33]

35. All too quickly, however, we forget the lessons of history, "the teacher of life."[34] Once this health crisis passes, our worst response would be to plunge even more deeply into feverish consumerism and new forms of egotistic self-preservation. God willing, after all this, we will think no longer in terms of "them" and "those," but only "us." If only this may prove not to be just another tragedy of history from which we learned nothing. If only we might keep in mind all those elderly persons who died for lack of respirators, partly as a result of the dismantling, year after year, of healthcare systems. If only this immense sorrow may not prove useless, but enable us to take a step forward towards a new style of life. If only we might rediscover once

---

[32] *Homily in Skopje, North Macedonia* (7 May 2019): *L'Osservatore Romano*, 8 May 2019, p. 12.

[33] Cf. *Aeneid* 1, 462: *"Sunt lacrimae rerum et mentem mortalia tangunt."*

[34] *"Historia... magistra vitae"* (CICERO, *De Oratore*, 2, 6).

for all that we need one another, and that in this way our human family can experience a rebirth, with all its faces, all its hands and all its voices, beyond the walls that we have erected.

36. Unless we recover the shared passion to create a community of belonging and solidarity worthy of our time, our energy and our resources, the global illusion that misled us will collapse and leave many in the grip of anguish and emptiness. Nor should we naively refuse to recognize that "obsession with a consumerist lifestyle, above all when few people are capable of maintaining it, can only lead to violence and mutual destruction."[35] The notion of "every man for himself" will rapidly degenerate into a free-for-all that would prove worse than any pandemic.

AN ABSENCE OF HUMAN DIGNITY ON THE BORDERS

37. Certain populist political regimes, as well as certain liberal economic approaches, maintain that an influx of migrants is to be prevented at all costs. Arguments are also made for the propriety of limiting aid to poor countries, so that they can hit rock bottom and find themselves forced to take austerity measures. One fails to realize that behind such statements, abstract and hard to support, great numbers of lives are at stake. Many migrants have fled from war, persecution and natural catastrophes. Others, rightly, "are seeking opportunities for themselves and their families. They dream of a better future and they want to create the conditions for achieving it."[36]

38. Sadly, some "are attracted by Western culture, sometimes with unrealistic expectations that expose them to grave

---

[35] Encyclical Letter *Laudato Si'* (24 May 2015), 204: AAS 107 (2015), 928.

[36] Post-Synodal Apostolic Exhortation *Christus Vivit* (25 March 2019), 91.

disappointments. Unscrupulous traffickers, frequently linked to drug cartels or arms cartels, exploit the weakness of migrants, who too often experience violence, trafficking, psychological and physical abuse and untold sufferings on their journey."[37] Those who emigrate "experience separation from their place of origin, and often a cultural and religious uprooting as well. Fragmentation is also felt by the communities they leave behind, which lose their most vigorous and enterprising elements, and by families, especially when one or both of the parents migrates, leaving the children in the country of origin."[38] For this reason, "there is also a need to reaffirm the right not to emigrate, that is, to remain in one's homeland."[39]

39. Then too, "in some host countries, migration causes fear and alarm, often fomented and exploited for political purposes. This can lead to a xenophobic mentality, as people close in on themselves, and it needs to be addressed decisively."[40] Migrants are not seen as entitled like others to participate in the life of society, and it is forgotten that they possess the same intrinsic dignity as any person. Hence they ought to be "agents in their own redemption."[41] No one will ever openly deny that they are human beings, yet in practice, by our decisions and the way we treat them, we can show that we consider them less worthy, less important, less human. For Christians, this way of thinking and acting is unacceptable, since it sets certain political preferences above deep convictions of our faith: the inalienable dignity of each human person regardless of origin, race or religion, and the supreme law of fraternal love.

---

[37] *Ibid.*, 92.

[38] *Ibid.*, 93.

[39] BENEDICT XVI, *Message for the 2013 World Day of Migrants and Refugees* (12 October 2012): AAS 104 (2012), 908.

[40] Post-Synodal Apostolic Exhortation *Christus Vivit* (25 March 2019), 92.

[41] *Message for the 2020 World Day of Migrants and Refugees* (13 May 2020): *L'Osservatore Romano*, 16 May 2020, p. 8.

40. "Migrations, more than ever before, will play a pivotal role in the future of our world."[42] At present, however, migration is affected by the "loss of that sense of responsibility for our brothers and sisters on which every civil society is based."[43] Europe, for example, seriously risks taking this path. Nonetheless, "aided by its great cultural and religious heritage, it has the means to defend the centrality of the human person and to find the right balance between its twofold moral responsibility to protect the rights of its citizens and to assure assistance and acceptance to migrants."[44]

41. I realize that some people are hesitant and fearful with regard to migrants. I consider this part of our natural instinct of self-defence. Yet it is also true that an individual and a people are only fruitful and productive if they are able to develop a creative openness to others. I ask everyone to move beyond those primal reactions because "there is a problem when doubts and fears condition our way of thinking and acting to the point of making us intolerant, closed and perhaps even – without realizing it – racist. In this way, fear deprives us of the desire and the ability to encounter the other."[45]

THE ILLUSION OF COMMUNICATION

42. Oddly enough, while closed and intolerant attitudes towards others are on the rise, distances are otherwise shrinking or disappearing to the point that the right to privacy scarcely exists. Everything has become a kind of spectacle to be examined and

---

[42] *Address to the Diplomatic Corps accredited to the Holy See* (11 January 2016): AAS 108 (2016), 124.

[43] *Address to the Diplomatic Corps accredited to the Holy See* (13 January 2014): AAS 106 (2014), 84.

[44] *Address to the Diplomatic Corps accredited to the Holy See* (11 January 2016): AAS 108 (2016), 123.

[45] *Message for the 2019 World Day of Migrants and Refugees* (27 May 2019): *L'Osservatore Romano*, 27-28 May 2019, p. 8.

inspected, and people's lives are now under constant surveillance. Digital communication wants to bring everything out into the open; people's lives are combed over, laid bare and bandied about, often anonymously. Respect for others disintegrates, and even as we dismiss, ignore or keep others distant, we can shamelessly peer into every detail of their lives.

42. Digital campaigns of hatred and destruction, for their part, are not – as some would have us believe – a positive form of mutual support, but simply an association of individuals united against a perceived common enemy. "Digital media can also expose people to the risk of addiction, isolation and a gradual loss of contact with concrete reality, blocking the development of authentic interpersonal relationships."[46] They lack the physical gestures, facial expressions, moments of silence, body language and even the smells, the trembling of hands, the blushes and perspiration that speak to us and are a part of human communication. Digital relationships, which do not demand the slow and gradual cultivation of friendships, stable interaction or the building of a consensus that matures over time, have the appearance of sociability. Yet they do not really build community; instead, they tend to disguise and expand the very individualism that finds expression in xenophobia and in contempt for the vulnerable. Digital connectivity is not enough to build bridges. It is not capable of uniting humanity.

Shameless aggression

44. Even as individuals maintain their comfortable consumerist isolation, they can choose a form of constant and febrile bonding that encourages remarkable hostility, insults, abuse, defamation and verbal violence destructive of others, and this with a lack of restraint that could not exist in physical contact without

---

[46] Post-Synodal Apostolic Exhortation *Christus Vivit* (25 March 2019), 88.

tearing us all apart. Social aggression has found unparalleled room for expansion through computers and mobile devices.

45. This has now given free rein to ideologies. Things that until a few years ago could not be said by anyone without risking the loss of universal respect can now be said with impunity, and in the crudest of terms, even by some political figures. Nor should we forget that "there are huge economic interests operating in the digital world, capable of exercising forms of control as subtle as they are invasive, creating mechanisms for the manipulation of consciences and of the democratic process. The way many platforms work often ends up favouring encounter between persons who think alike, shielding them from debate. These closed circuits facilitate the spread of fake news and false information, fomenting prejudice and hate."[47]

46. We should also recognize that destructive forms of fanaticism are at times found among religious believers, including Christians; they too "can be caught up in networks of verbal violence through the internet and the various forums of digital communication. Even in Catholic media, limits can be overstepped, defamation and slander can become commonplace, and all ethical standards and respect for the good name of others can be abandoned."[48] How can this contribute to the fraternity that our common Father asks of us?

Information without wisdom

47. True wisdom demands an encounter with reality. Today, however, everything can be created, disguised and altered. A direct encounter even with the fringes of reality can thus prove intolerable. A mechanism of selection then comes into play, whereby I can immediately separate likes from dislikes, what I consider attractive from what I deem distasteful. In the

---

[47] Ibid., 89.
[48] Apostolic Exhortation *Gaudete et Exsultate* (19 March 2018), 115.

same way, we can choose the people with whom we wish to share our world. Persons or situations we find unpleasant or disagreeable are simply deleted in today's virtual networks; a virtual circle is then created, isolating us from the real world in which we are living.

48. The ability to sit down and listen to others, typical of inter-personal encounters, is paradigmatic of the welcoming attitude shown by those who transcend narcissism and accept others, caring for them and welcoming them into their lives. Yet "to-day's world is largely a deaf world... At times, the frantic pace of the modern world prevents us from listening attentively to what another person is saying. Halfway through, we interrupt him and want to contradict what he has not even finished say-ing. We must not lose our ability to listen." Saint Francis "heard the voice of God, he heard the voice of the poor, he heard the voice of the infirm and he heard the voice of nature. He made of them a way of life. My desire is that the seed that Saint Francis planted may grow in the hearts of many."[49]

49. As silence and careful listening disappear, replaced by a frenzy of texting, this basic structure of sage human commu-nication is at risk. A new lifestyle is emerging, where we create only what we want and exclude all that we cannot control or know instantly and superficially. This process, by its intrinsic logic, blocks the kind of serene reflection that could lead us to a shared wisdom.

50. Together, we can seek the truth in dialogue, in relaxed conversation or in passionate debate. To do so calls for perse-verance; it entails moments of silence and suffering, yet it can patiently embrace the broader experience of individuals and peoples. The flood of information at our fingertips does not make for greater wisdom. Wisdom is not born of quick searches

---

[49] From the film *Pope Francis: A Man of His Word*, by Wim Wenders (2018).

on the internet nor is it a mass of unverified data. That is not the way to mature in the encounter with truth. Conversations revolve only around the latest data; they become merely horizontal and cumulative. We fail to keep our attention focused, to penetrate to the heart of matters, and to recognize what is essential to give meaning to our lives. Freedom thus becomes an illusion that we are peddled, easily confused with the ability to navigate the internet. The process of building fraternity, be it local or universal, can only be undertaken by spirits that are free and open to authentic encounters.

FORMS OF SUBJECTION AND OF SELF-CONTEMPT

51. Certain economically prosperous countries tend to be proposed as cultural models for less developed countries; instead, each of those countries should be helped to grow in its own distinct way and to develop its capacity for innovation while respecting the values of its proper culture. A shallow and pathetic desire to imitate others leads to copying and consuming in place of creating, and fosters low national self-esteem. In the affluent sectors of many poor countries, and at times in those who have recently emerged from poverty, there is a resistance to native ways of thinking and acting, and a tendency to look down on one's own cultural identity, as if it were the sole cause of every ill.

52. Destroying self-esteem is an easy way to dominate others. Behind these trends that tend to level our world, there flourish powerful interests that take advantage of such low self-esteem, while attempting, through the media and networks, to create a new culture in the service of the elite. This plays into the opportunism of financial speculators and raiders, and the poor always end up the losers. Then too, ignoring the culture of their people has led to the inability of many political leaders to devise an effective development plan that could be freely accepted and sustained over time.

53. We forget that "there is no worse form of alienation than to feel uprooted, belonging to no one. A land will be fruitful, and its people bear fruit and give birth to the future, only to the extent that it can foster a sense of belonging among its members, create bonds of integration between generations and different communities, and avoid all that makes us insensitive to others and leads to further alienation."[50]

HOPE

54. Despite these dark clouds, which may not be ignored, I would like in the following pages to take up and discuss many new paths of hope. For God continues to sow abundant seeds of goodness in our human family. The recent pandemic enabled us to recognize and appreciate once more all those around us who, in the midst of fear, responded by putting their lives on the line. We began to realize that our lives are interwoven with and sustained by ordinary people valiantly shaping the decisive events of our shared history: doctors, nurses, pharmacists, storekeepers and supermarket workers, cleaning personnel, caretakers, transport workers, men and women working to provide essential services and public safety, volunteers, priests and religious... They understood that no one is saved alone.[51]

55. I invite everyone to renewed hope, for hope "speaks to us of something deeply rooted in every human heart, independently of our circumstances and historical conditioning. Hope speaks to us of a thirst, an aspiration, a longing for a life of fulfillment, a desire to achieve great things, things that fill our heart and

---

[50] *Address to Authorities, Civil Society and the Diplomatic Corps*, Tallinn, Estonia (25 September 2018): *L'Osservatore Romano*, 27 September 2018, p. 7.
[51] Cf. *Extraordinary Moment of Prayer in Time of Epidemic* (27 March 2020): *L'Osservatore Romano*, 29 March 2020, p. 10; *Message for the 2020 World Day of the Poor* (13 June 2020), 6: *L'Osservatore Romano*, 14 June 2020, p. 8.

lift our spirit to lofty realities like truth, goodness and beauty, justice and love... Hope is bold; it can look beyond personal convenience, the petty securities and compensations which limit our horizon, and it can open us up to grand ideals that make life more beautiful and worthwhile."[52] Let us continue, then, to advance along the paths of hope.

CHAPTER TWO

A STRANGER ON THE ROAD

56. The previous chapter should not be read as a cool and detached description of today's problems, for "the joys and hopes, the grief and anguish of the people of our time, especially of those who are poor or afflicted, are the joys and hopes, the grief and anguish of the followers of Christ as well. Nothing that is genuinely human fails to find an echo in their hearts."[53] In the attempt to search for a ray of light in the midst of what we are experiencing, and before proposing a few lines of action, I now wish to devote a chapter to a parable told by Jesus Christ two thousand years ago. Although this Letter is addressed to all people of good will, regardless of their religious convictions, the parable is one that any of us can relate to and find challenging.

"Just then a lawyer stood up to test Jesus. 'Teacher,' he said, 'what must I do to inherit eternal life?' He said to him, 'What is written in the law? What do you read there?' He answered, 'You shall love the Lord your God with all your heart, and with all your soul, and with all your strength, and with all your mind;

---

[52] *Greeting to Young People at the Padre Félix Varela Cultural Centre*, Havana, Cuba (20 September 2015): *L'Osservatore Romano*, 21-22 September 2015, p. 6.

[53] SECOND VATICAN ECUMENICAL COUNCIL, Pastoral Constitution on the Church in the Modern World *Gaudium et Spes*, 1.

and your neighbour as yourself.' And he said to him, 'You have given the right answer; do this, and you will live.' But wanting to justify himself, he asked Jesus, 'And who is my neighbour?' Jesus replied, 'A man was going down from Jerusalem to Jericho, and fell into the hands of robbers, who stripped him, beat him, and went away, leaving him half dead. Now by chance a priest was going down that road; and when he saw him, he passed by on the other side. So likewise a Levite, when he came to the place and saw him, passed by on the other side. But a Samaritan while traveling came near him; and when he saw him, he was moved with pity. He went to him and bandaged his wounds, having poured oil and wine on them. Then he put him on his own animal, brought him to an inn, and took care of him. The next day he took out two denarii, gave them to the innkeeper, and said, 'Take care of him; and when I come back, I will repay you whatever more you spend.' Which of these three, do you think, was a neighbour to the man who fell into the hands of the robbers?" He said, 'The one who showed him mercy.' Jesus said to him, 'Go and do likewise.'"(Lk 10:25-37).

The context

57. This parable has to do with an age-old problem. Shortly after its account of the creation of the world and of man, the Bible takes up the issue of human relationships. Cain kills his brother Abel and then hears God ask: "Where is your brother Abel?" (*Gen* 4:9). His answer is one that we ourselves all too often give: "Am I my brother's keeper?" (ibid.). By the very question he asks, God leaves no room for an appeal to determinism or fatalism as a justification for our own indifference. Instead, he encourages us to create a different culture, in which we resolve our conflicts and care for one another.

58. The Book of Job sees our origin in the one Creator as the basis of certain common rights: "Did not he who made me in

the womb also make him? And did not the same one fashion us in the womb?" (*Job* 31:15). Many centuries later, Saint Irenaeus would use the image of a melody to make the same point: "One who seeks the truth should not concentrate on the differences between one note and another, thinking as if each was created separately and apart from the others; instead, he should realize that one and the same person composed the entire melody."[54]

59. In earlier Jewish traditions, the imperative to love and care for others appears to have been limited to relationships between members of the same nation. The ancient commandment to "love your neighbour as yourself" (*Lev* 19:18) was usually understood as referring to one's fellow citizens, yet the boundaries gradually expanded, especially in the Judaism that developed outside of the land of Israel. We encounter the command not to do to others what you would not want them to do to you (cf. *Tob* 4:15). In the first century before Christ, Rabbi Hillel stated: "This is the entire Torah. Everything else is commentary."[55] The desire to imitate God's own way of acting gradually replaced the tendency to think only of those nearest us: "The compassion of man is for his neighbour, but the compassion of the Lord is for all living beings" (*Sir* 18:13).

60. In the New Testament, Hillel's precept was expressed in positive terms: "In everything, do to others as you would have them do to you; for this is the law and the prophets" (*Mt* 7:12). This command is universal in scope, embracing everyone on the basis of our shared humanity, since the heavenly Father "makes his sun rise on the evil and on the good" (*Mt* 5:45). Hence the summons to "be merciful, just as your Father is merciful" (*Lk* 6:36).

---

[54] SAINT IRENAEUS OF LYONS, *Adversus Haereses*, II, 25, 2: PG 7/1, 798ff.

[55] *Talmud Bavli* (Babylonian Talmud), *Shabbat*, 31a.

61. In the oldest texts of the Bible, we find a reason why our hearts should expand to embrace the foreigner. It derives from the enduring memory of the Jewish people that they themselves had once lived as foreigners in Egypt:

"You shall not wrong or oppress a stranger, for you were strangers in the land of Egypt" (*Ex* 22:21).

"You shall not oppress a stranger; you know the heart of a stranger, for you were strangers in the land of Egypt" (*Ex* 23:9).

"When a stranger resides with you in your land, you shall not do him wrong. The stranger who resides with you shall be to you as the citizen among you; you shall love the stranger as yourself, for you were strangers in the land of Egypt" (*Lev* 19:33-34).

"When you gather the grapes of your vineyard, do not glean what is left; it shall be for the sojourner, the orphan, and the widow. Remember that you were a slave in the land of Egypt" (*Deut* 24:21-22).

The call to fraternal love echoes throughout the New Testament:

"For the whole law is summed up in a single commandment, 'You shall love your neighbour as yourself'" (*Gal* 5:14).

"Whoever loves a brother or sister lives in the light, and in such a person there is no cause for stumbling. But whoever hates another believer is in the darkness" (*1 Jn* 2:10-11).

"We know that we have passed from death to life because we love one another. Whoever does not love abides in death" (*1 Jn* 3:14).

"Those who do not love a brother or sister whom they have seen, cannot love God whom they have not seen" (*1 Jn* 4:20).

62. Yet this call to love could be misunderstood. Saint Paul, recognizing the temptation of the earliest Christian communities to form closed and isolated groups, urged his disciples to abound in love "for one another and for all" (*1 Thess* 3:12). In the Johannine community, fellow Christians were to be welcomed, "even though they are strangers to you" (*3 Jn* 5). In this context, we can better understand the significance of the parable of the Good Samaritan: love does not care if a brother or sister in need comes from one place or another. For "love shatters the chains that keep us isolated and separate; in their place, it builds bridges. Love enables us to create one great family, where all of us can feel at home... Love exudes compassion and dignity."[56]

Abandoned on the wayside

63. Jesus tells the story of a man assaulted by thieves and lying injured on the wayside. Several persons passed him by, but failed to stop. These were people holding important social positions, yet lacking in real concern for the common good. They would not waste a couple of minutes caring for the injured man, or even in calling for help. Only one person stopped, approached the man and cared for him personally, even spending his own money to provide for his needs. He also gave him something that in our frenetic world we cling to tightly: he gave him his time. Certainly, he had his own plans for that day, his own needs, commitments and desires. Yet he was able to put all that aside when confronted with someone in need. Without even knowing the injured man, he saw him as deserving of his time and attention.

64. Which of these persons do you identify with? This question, blunt as it is, is direct and incisive. Which of these characters do you resemble? We need to acknowledge that we are constantly

---

[56] *Address to Those Assisted by the Charitable Works of the Church*, Tallinn, Estonia (25 September 2018): *L'Osservatore Romano*, 27 September 2018, p. 8.

tempted to ignore others, especially the weak. Let us admit that, for all the progress we have made, we are still "illiterate" when it comes to accompanying, caring for and supporting the most frail and vulnerable members of our developed societies. We have become accustomed to looking the other way, passing by, ignoring situations until they affect us directly.

65. Someone is assaulted on our streets, and many hurry off as if they did not notice. People hit someone with their car and then flee the scene. Their only desire is to avoid problems; it does not matter that, through their fault, another person could die. All these are signs of an approach to life that is spreading in various and subtle ways. What is more, caught up as we are with our own needs, the sight of a person who is suffering disturbs us. It makes us uneasy, since we have no time to waste on other people's problems. These are symptoms of an unhealthy society. A society that seeks prosperity but turns its back on suffering.

66. May we not sink to such depths! Let us look to the example of the Good Samaritan. Jesus' parable summons us to rediscover our vocation as citizens of our respective nations and of the entire world, builders of a new social bond. This summons is ever new, yet it is grounded in a fundamental law of our being: we are called to direct society to the pursuit of the common good and, with this purpose in mind, to persevere in consolidating its political and social order, its fabric of relations, its human goals. By his actions, the Good Samaritan showed that "the existence of each and every individual is deeply tied to that of others: life is not simply time that passes; life is a time for interactions."[57]

67. The parable eloquently presents the basic decision we need to make in order to rebuild our wounded world. In the face of

---

[57] *Video Message to the TED Conference in Vancouver* (26 April 2017):*L'Osservatore Romano*, 27 April 2017, p. 7.

so much pain and suffering, our only course is to imitate the Good Samaritan. Any other decision would make us either one of the robbers or one of those who walked by without showing compassion for the sufferings of the man on the roadside. The parable shows us how a community can be rebuilt by men and women who identify with the vulnerability of others, who reject the creation of a society of exclusion, and act instead as neighbours, lifting up and rehabilitating the fallen for the sake of the common good. At the same time, it warns us about the attitude of those who think only of themselves and fail to shoulder the inevitable responsibilities of life as it is.

68. The parable clearly does not indulge in abstract moralizing, nor is its message merely social and ethical. It speaks to us of an essential and often forgotten aspect of our common humanity: we were created for a fulfilment that can only be found in love. We cannot be indifferent to suffering; we cannot allow anyone to go through life as an outcast. Instead, we should feel indignant, challenged to emerge from our comfortable isolation and to be changed by our contact with human suffering. That is the meaning of dignity.

A story constantly retold

69. The parable is clear and straightforward, yet it also evokes the interior struggle that each of us experiences as we gradually come to know ourselves through our relationships with our brothers and sisters. Sooner or later, we will all encounter a person who is suffering. Today there are more and more of them. The decision to include or exclude those lying wounded along the roadside can serve as a criterion for judging every economic, political, social and religious project. Each day we have to decide whether to be Good Samaritans or indifferent bystanders. And if we extend our gaze to the history of our own lives and that of the entire world, all of us are, or have been, like each of the characters in the parable. All of us have

in ourselves something of the wounded man, something of the robber, something of the passers-by, and something of the Good Samaritan.

70. It is remarkable how the various characters in the story change, once confronted by the painful sight of the poor man on the roadside. The distinctions between Judean and Samaritan, priest and merchant, fade into insignificance. Now there are only two kinds of people: those who care for someone who is hurting and those who pass by; those who bend down to help and those who look the other way and hurry off. Here, all our distinctions, labels and masks fall away: it is the moment of truth. Will we bend down to touch and heal the wounds of others? Will we bend down and help another to get up? This is today's challenge, and we should not be afraid to face it. In moments of crisis, decisions become urgent. It could be said that, here and now, anyone who is neither a robber nor a passer-by is either injured himself or bearing an injured person on his shoulders.

71. The story of the Good Samaritan is constantly being repeated. We can see this clearly as social and political inertia is turning many parts of our world into a desolate byway, even as domestic and international disputes and the robbing of opportunities are leaving great numbers of the marginalized stranded on the roadside. In his parable, Jesus does not offer alternatives; he does not ask what might have happened had the injured man or the one who helped him yielded to anger or a thirst for revenge. Jesus trusts in the best of the human spirit; with this parable, he encourages us to persevere in love, to restore dignity to the suffering and to build a society worthy of the name.

The characters of the story

72. The parable begins with the robbers. Jesus chose to start when the robbery has already taken place, lest we dwell on

the crime itself or the thieves who committed it. Yet we know them well. We have seen, descending on our world, the dark shadows of neglect and violence in the service of petty interests of power, gain and division. The real question is this: will we abandon the injured man and run to take refuge from the violence, or will we pursue the thieves? Will the wounded man end up being the justification for our irreconcilable divisions, our cruel indifference, our intestine conflicts?

73. The parable then asks us to take a closer look at the passers-by. The nervous indifference that makes them pass to the other side of the road – whether innocently or not, whether the result of disdain or mere distraction – makes the priest and the Levite a sad reflection of the growing gulf between ourselves and the world around us. There are many ways to pass by at a safe distance: we can retreat inwards, ignore others, or be indifferent to their plight. Or simply look elsewhere, as in some countries, or certain sectors of them, where contempt is shown for the poor and their culture, and one looks the other way, as if a development plan imported from without could edge them out. This is how some justify their indifference: the poor, whose pleas for help might touch their hearts, simply do not exist. The poor are beyond the scope of their interest.

74. One detail about the passers-by does stand out: they were religious, devoted to the worship of God: a priest and a Levite. This detail should not be overlooked. It shows that belief in God and the worship of God are not enough to ensure that we are actually living in a way pleasing to God. A believer may be untrue to everything that his faith demands of him, and yet think he is close to God and better than others. The guarantee of an authentic openness to God, on the other hand, is a way of practising the faith that helps open our hearts to our brothers and sisters. Saint John Chrysostom expressed this pointedly when he challenged his Christian hearers: "Do you wish to honour the body of the Saviour? Do not despise it when it is

naked. Do not honour it in church with silk vestments while outside it is naked and numb with cold."[58] Paradoxically, those who claim to be unbelievers can sometimes put God's will into practice better than believers.

75. "Robbers" usually find secret allies in those who "pass by and look the other way." There is a certain interplay between those who manipulate and cheat society, and those who, while claiming to be detached and impartial critics, live off that system and its benefits. There is a sad hypocrisy when the impunity of crime, the use of institutions for personal or corporate gain, and other evils apparently impossible to eradicate, are accompanied by a relentless criticism of everything, a constant sowing of suspicion that results in distrust and confusion. The complaint that "everything is broken" is answered by the claim that "it can't be fixed," or "what can I do?" This feeds into disillusionment and despair, and hardly encourages a spirit of solidarity and generosity. Plunging people into despair closes a perfectly perverse circle: such is the agenda of the invisible dictatorship of hidden interests that have gained mastery over both resources and the possibility of thinking and expressing opinions.

76. Let us turn at last to the injured man. There are times when we feel like him, badly hurt and left on side of the road. We can also feel helpless because our institutions are neglected and lack resources, or simply serve the interests of a few, without and within. Indeed, "globalized society often has an elegant way of shifting its gaze. Under the guise of being politically correct or ideologically fashionable, we look at those who suffer without touching them. We televise live pictures of them, even speaking about them with euphemisms and with apparent tolerance."[59]

---

[58] *Homiliae in Matthaeum*, 50: 3-4: PG 58, 508.

[59] *Message to the Meeting of Popular Movements*, Modesto, California, United States of America (10 February 2017): AAS 109 (2017), 291.

Starting anew

77. Each day offers us a new opportunity, a new possibility. We should not expect everything from those who govern us, for that would be childish. We have the space we need for co-responsibility in creating and putting into place new processes and changes. Let us take an active part in renewing and supporting our troubled societies. Today we have a great opportunity to express our innate sense of fraternity, to be Good Samaritans who bear the pain of other people's troubles rather than fomenting greater hatred and resentment. Like the chance traveller in the parable, we need only have a pure and simple desire to be a people, a community, constant and tireless in the effort to include, integrate and lift up the fallen. We may often find ourselves succumbing to the mentality of the violent, the blindly ambitious, those who spread mistrust and lies. Others may continue to view politics or the economy as an arena for their own power plays. For our part, let us foster what is good and place ourselves at its service.

78. We can start from below and, case by case, act at the most concrete and local levels, and then expand to the farthest reaches of our countries and our world, with the same care and concern that the Samaritan showed for each of the wounded man's injuries. Let us seek out others and embrace the world as it is, without fear of pain or a sense of inadequacy, because there we will discover all the goodness that God has planted in human hearts. Difficulties that seem overwhelming are opportunities for growth, not excuses for a glum resignation that can lead only to acquiescence. Yet let us not do this alone, as individuals. The Samaritan discovered an innkeeper who would care for the man; we too are called to unite as a family that is stronger than the sum of small individual members. For "the whole is greater than the part, but it is also greater than the sum of its parts."[60] Let us

---

[60] Apostolic Exhortation *Evangelii Gaudium* (24 November 2013), 235: AAS 105 (2013), 1115.

renounce the pettiness and resentment of useless in-fighting and constant confrontation. Let us stop feeling sorry for ourselves and acknowledge our crimes, our apathy, our lies. Reparation and reconciliation will give us new life and set us all free from fear.

79. The Samaritan who stopped along the way departed without expecting any recognition or gratitude. His effort to assist another person gave him great satisfaction in life and before his God, and thus became a duty. All of us have a responsibility for the wounded, those of our own people and all the peoples of the earth. Let us care for the needs of every man and woman, young and old, with the same fraternal spirit of care and closeness that marked the Good Samaritan.

Neighbours without borders

80. Jesus told the parable of the Good Samaritan in answer to the question: Who is my neighbour? The word "neighbour," in the society of Jesus' time, usually meant those nearest us. It was felt that help should be given primarily to those of one's own group and race. For some Jews of that time, Samaritans were looked down upon, considered impure. They were not among those to be helped. Jesus, himself a Jew, completely transforms this approach. He asks us not to decide who is close enough to be our neighbour, but rather that we ourselves become neighbours to all.

81. Jesus asks us to be present to those in need of help, regardless of whether or not they belong to our social group. In this case, the Samaritan *became a neighbour* to the wounded Judean. By approaching and making himself present, he crossed all cultural and historical barriers. Jesus concludes the parable by saying: "Go and do likewise" (*Lk* 10:37). In other words, he challenges us to put aside all differences and, in the face of suffering, to draw near to others with no questions asked. I should no longer say that I have neighbours to help, but that I must myself be a neighbour to others.

82. The parable, though, is troubling, for Jesus says that that the wounded man was a Judean, while the one who stopped and helped him was a Samaritan. This detail is quite significant for our reflection on a love that includes everyone. The Samaritans lived in a region where pagan rites were practised. For the Jews, this made them impure, detestable, dangerous. In fact, one ancient Jewish text referring to nations that were hated, speaks of Samaria as "not even a people" (*Sir* 50:25); it also refers to "the foolish people that live in Shechem" (50:26).

83. This explains why a Samaritan woman, when asked by Jesus for a drink, answered curtly: "How is it that you, a Jew, ask a drink of me, a woman of Samaria?" (*Jn* 4:9). The most offensive charge that those who sought to discredit Jesus could bring was that he was "possessed" and "a Samaritan" (*Jn* 8:48). So this encounter of mercy between a Samaritan and a Jew is highly provocative; it leaves no room for ideological manipulation and challenges us to expand our frontiers. It gives a universal dimension to our call to love, one that transcends all prejudices, all historical and cultural barriers, all petty interests.

The plea of the stranger

84. Finally, I would note that in another passage of the Gospel Jesus says: "I was a stranger and you welcomed me" (*Mt* 25:35). Jesus could speak those words because he had an open heart, sensitive to the difficulties of others. Saint Paul urges us to "rejoice with those who rejoice, weep with those who weep" (*Rom* 12:15). When our hearts do this, they are capable of identifying with others without worrying about where they were born or come from. In the process, we come to experience others as our "own flesh" (*Is* 58:7).

85. For Christians, the words of Jesus have an even deeper meaning. They compel us to recognize Christ himself in each of our abandoned or excluded brothers and sisters

(cf. *Mt* 25:40.45). Faith has untold power to inspire and sustain our respect for others, for believers come to know that God loves every man and woman with infinite love and "thereby confers infinite dignity" upon all humanity.[61] We likewise believe that Christ shed his blood for each of us and that no one is beyond the scope of his universal love. If we go to the ultimate source of that love which is the very life of the triune God, we encounter in the community of the three divine Persons the origin and perfect model of all life in society. Theology continues to be enriched by its reflection on this great truth.

86. I sometimes wonder why, in light of this, it took so long for the Church unequivocally to condemn slavery and various forms of violence. Today, with our developed spirituality and theology, we have no excuses. Still, there are those who appear to feel encouraged or at least permitted by their faith to support varieties of narrow and violent nationalism, xenophobia and contempt, and even the mistreatment of those who are different. Faith, and the humanism it inspires, must maintain a critical sense in the face of these tendencies, and prompt an immediate response whenever they rear their head. For this reason, it is important that catechesis and preaching speak more directly and clearly about the social meaning of existence, the fraternal dimension of spirituality, our conviction of the inalienable dignity of each person, and our reasons for loving and accepting all our brothers and sisters.

CHAPTER THREE

ENVISAGING AND ENGENDERING AN OPEN WORLD

87. Human beings are so made that they cannot live, develop and find fulfilment except "in the sincere gift of self to

---

[61] SAINT JOHN PAUL II, *Message to the Handicapped, Angelus* in Osnabrück, Germany (16 November 1980): *Insegnamenti* III, 2 (1980), 1232.

others."[62] Nor can they fully know themselves apart from an encounter with other persons: "I communicate effectively with myself only insofar as I communicate with others."[63] No one can experience the true beauty of life without relating to others, without having real faces to love. This is part of the mystery of authentic human existence. "Life exists where there is bonding, communion, fraternity; and life is stronger than death when it is built on true relationships and bonds of fidelity. On the contrary, there is no life when we claim to be self-sufficient and live as islands: in these attitudes, death prevails."[64]

MOVING BEYOND OURSELVES

88. In the depths of every heart, love creates bonds and expands existence, for it draws people out of themselves and towards others.[65] Since we were made for love, in each one of us "a law of *ekstasis*" seems to operate: "the lover 'goes outside' the self to find a fuller existence in another."[66] For this reason, "man always has to take up the challenge of moving beyond himself."[67]

89. Nor can I reduce my life to relationships with a small group, even my own family; I cannot know myself apart from a broader network of relationships, including those that have preceded me and shaped my entire life. My relationship with those whom I respect has to take account of the fact that they do not live only for me, nor do I live only for them. Our relationships,

[62] SECOND VATICAN ECUMENICAL COUNCIL, Pastoral Constitution on the Church in the Modern World *Gaudium et Spes*, 24.

[63] Gabriel Marcel, *Du refus à l'invocation*, ed. NRF, Paris, 1940, 50.

[64] *Angelus* (10 November 2019): *L'Osservatore Romano*, 11-12 November 2019, 8.

[65] Cf. Saint Thomas Aquinas: *Scriptum super Sententiis*, lib. 3, dist. 27, q. 1, a. 1, ad 4: "Dicitur amor extasim facere et fervere, quia quod fervet extra se bullit et exhalat."

[66] Karol Wojtyła, *Love and Responsibility*, London, 1982, 126.

[67] Karl Rahner, *Kleines Kirchenjahr. Ein Gang durch den Festkreis*, Herderbücherei 901, Freiburg, 1981, 30.

if healthy and authentic, open us to others who expand and enrich us. Nowadays, our noblest social instincts can easily be thwarted by self-centred chats that give the impression of being deep relationships. On the contrary, authentic and mature love and true friendship can only take root in hearts open to growth through relationships with others. As couples or friends, we find that our hearts expand as we step out of ourselves and embrace others. Closed groups and self-absorbed couples that define themselves in opposition to others tend to be expressions of selfishness and mere self-preservation.

90. Significantly, many small communities living in desert areas developed a remarkable system of welcoming pilgrims as an exercise of the sacred duty of hospitality. The medieval monastic communities did likewise, as we see from the Rule of Saint Benedict. While acknowledging that it might detract from the discipline and silence of monasteries, Benedict nonetheless insisted that "the poor and pilgrims be treated with the utmost care and attention."[68] Hospitality was one specific way of rising to the challenge and the gift present in an encounter with those outside one's own circle. The monks realized that the values they sought to cultivate had to be accompanied by a readiness to move beyond themselves in openness to others.

The unique value of love

91. People can develop certain habits that might appear as moral values: fortitude, sobriety, hard work and similar virtues. Yet if the acts of the various moral virtues are to be rightly directed, one needs to take into account the extent to which they foster openness and union with others. That is made possible by the charity that God infuses. Without charity, we may perhaps possess only apparent virtues, incapable of sustaining life in common. Thus, Saint Thomas Aquinas

---

[68] *Regula*, 53, 15: *"Pauperum et peregrinorum maxime susceptioni cura sollicite exhibeatur."*

could say – quoting Saint Augustine – that the temperance of a greedy person is in no way virtuous.[69] Saint Bonaventure, for his part, explained that the other virtues, without charity, strictly speaking do not fulfil the commandments "the way God wants them to be fulfilled."[70]

92. The spiritual stature of a person's life is measured by love, which in the end remains "the criterion for the definitive decision about a human life's worth or lack thereof."[71] Yet some believers think that it consists in the imposition of their own ideologies upon everyone else, or in a violent defence of the truth, or in impressive demonstrations of strength. All of us, as believers, need to recognize that love takes first place: love must never be put at risk, and the greatest danger lies in failing to love (cf. *1 Cor* 13:1-13).

93. Saint Thomas Aquinas sought to describe the love made possible by God's grace as a movement outwards towards another, whereby we consider "the beloved as somehow united to ourselves."[72] Our affection for others makes us freely desire to seek their good. All this originates in a sense of esteem, an appreciation of the value of the other. This is ultimately the idea behind the word "charity": those who are loved are "dear" to me; "they are considered of great value."[73] And "the love whereby someone becomes pleasing (*grata*) to another is the reason why the latter bestows something on him freely (*gratis*)."[74]

---

[69] Cf. *Summa Theologiae*, II-II, q. 23, a. 7; Saint Augustine, *Contra Julianum*, 4, 18: PL 44, 748: "How many pleasures do misers forego, either to increase their treasures or for fear of seeing them diminish!."

[70] *"Secundum acceptionem divinam"* (*Scriptum super Sententiis*, lib. 3, dist. 27, a. 1, q. 1, concl. 4).

[71] Benedict XVI, Encyclical Letter *Deus Caritas Est* (25 December 2005), 15: AAS 98 (2006), 230.

[72] *Summa Theologiae* II-II, q. 27, a. 2, resp.

[73] Cf. ibid., I-II, q. 26, a. 3, resp.

[74] Ibid., q. 110, a. 1, resp.

94. Love, then, is more than just a series of benevolent actions. Those actions have their source in a union increasingly directed towards others, considering them of value, worthy, pleasing and beautiful apart from their physical or moral appearances. Our love for others, for who they *are*, moves us to seek the best for their lives. Only by cultivating this way of relating to one another will we make possible a social friendship that excludes no one and a fraternity that is open to all.

A LOVE EVER MORE OPEN

95. Love also impels us towards universal communion. No one can mature or find fulfilment by withdrawing from others. By its very nature, love calls for growth in openness and the ability to accept others as part of a continuing adventure that makes every periphery converge in a greater sense of mutual belonging. As Jesus told us: "You are all brothers" (*Mt* 23:8).

96. This need to transcend our own limitations also applies to different regions and countries. Indeed, "the ever-increasing number of interconnections and communications in today's world makes us powerfully aware of the unity and common destiny of the nations. In the dynamics of history, and in the diversity of ethnic groups, societies and cultures, we see the seeds of a vocation to form a community composed of brothers and sisters who accept and care for one another."[75]

Open societies that integrate everyone

97. Some peripheries are close to us, in city centres or within our families. Hence there is an aspect of universal openness in love that is existential rather than geographical. It has to do with our daily efforts to expand our circle of friends, to reach those who, even though they are close to me, I do not naturally

---

[75] *Message for the 2014 World Day of Peace* (8 December 2013), 1: AAS 106 (2014), 22.

consider a part of my circle of interests. Every brother or sister in need, when abandoned or ignored by the society in which I live, becomes an existential foreigner, even though born in the same country. They may be citizens with full rights, yet they are treated like foreigners in their own country. Racism is a virus that quickly mutates and, instead of disappearing, goes into hiding, and lurks in waiting.

98. I would like to mention some of those "hidden exiles" who are treated as foreign bodies in society.[76] Many persons with disabilities "feel that they exist without belonging and without participating." Much still prevents them from being fully enfranchised. Our concern should be not only to care for them but to ensure their "active participation in the civil and ecclesial community. That is a demanding and even tiring process, yet one that will gradually contribute to the formation of consciences capable of acknowledging each individual as a unique and unrepeatable person." I think, too, of "the elderly who, also due to their disability, are sometimes considered a burden." Yet each of them is able to offer "a unique contribution to the common good through their remarkable life stories." Let me repeat: we need to have "the courage to give a voice to those who are discriminated against due to their disability, because sadly, in some countries even today, people find it hard to acknowledge them as persons of equal dignity."[77]

Inadequate understandings of universal love

99. A love capable of transcending borders is the basis of what in every city and country can be called "social friendship." Genuine social friendship within a society makes true universal

---

[76] Cf. *Angelus* (29 December 2013): *L'Osservatore Romano,* 30-31 December 2013, p. 7; *Address to the Diplomatic Corps Accredited to the Holy See* (12 January 2015): AAS 107 (2015), 165.

[77] *Message for the World Day of Persons with Disabilities* (3 December 2019): *L'Osservatore Romano,* 4 December 2019, 7.

openness possible. This is a far cry from the false universalism of those who constantly travel abroad because they cannot tolerate or love their own people. Those who look down on their own people tend to create within society categories of first and second class, people of greater or lesser dignity, people enjoying greater or fewer rights. In this way, they deny that there is room for everybody.

100. I am certainly not proposing an authoritarian and abstract universalism, devised or planned by a small group and presented as an ideal for the sake of levelling, dominating and plundering. One model of globalization in fact "consciously aims at a one-dimensional uniformity and seeks to eliminate all differences and traditions in a superficial quest for unity… If a certain kind of globalization claims to make everyone uniform, to level everyone out, that globalization destroys the rich gifts and uniqueness of each person and each people."[78] This false universalism ends up depriving the world of its various colours, its beauty and, ultimately, its humanity. For "the future is not monochrome; if we are courageous, we can contemplate it in all the variety and diversity of what each individual person has to offer. How much our human family needs to learn to live together in harmony and peace, without all of us having to be the same!"[79]

BEYOND A WORLD OF "ASSOCIATES"

101. Let us now return to the parable of the Good Samaritan, for it still has much to say to us. An injured man lay on the roadside. The people walking by him did not heed their interior summons to act as neighbours; they were concerned with their

---

[78] *Address to the Meeting for Religious Liberty with the Hispanic Community and Immigrant Groups*, Philadelphia, Pennsylvania, United States of America (26 September 2015): AAS 107 (2015), 1050-1051.

[79] *Address to Young People*, Tokyo, Japan (25 November 2019): *L'Osservatore Romano,* 25-26 November 2019, 10.

duties, their social status, their professional position within society. They considered themselves important for the society of the time, and were anxious to play their proper part. The man on the roadside, bruised and abandoned, was a distraction, an interruption from all that; in any event, he was hardly important. He was a "nobody," undistinguished, irrelevant to their plans for the future. The Good Samaritan transcended these narrow classifications. He himself did not fit into any of those categories; he was simply a foreigner without a place in society. Free of every label and position, he was able to interrupt his journey, change his plans, and unexpectedly come to the aid of an injured person who needed his help.

102. What would be the reaction to that same story nowadays, in a world that constantly witnesses the emergence and growth of social groups clinging to an identity that separates them from others? How would it affect those who organize themselves in a way that prevents any foreign presence that might threaten their identity and their closed and self-referential structures? There, even the possibility of acting as a neighbour is excluded; one is a neighbour only to those who serve their purpose. The word "neighbour" loses all meaning; there can only be "associates," partners in the pursuit of particular interests.[80]

Liberty, equality and fraternity

103. Fraternity is born not only of a climate of respect for individual liberties, or even of a certain administratively guaranteed equality. Fraternity necessarily calls for something greater, which in turn enhances freedom and equality. What happens when fraternity is not consciously cultivated, when there is a lack of political will to promote it through education in fraternity, through dialogue and through the recognition of the values

---

[80] In these considerations, I have been inspired by the thought of Paul Ricoeur, "Le socius et le prochain," in *Histoire et Verité*, ed. Le Seuil, Paris, 1967, 113-127.

of reciprocity and mutual enrichment? Liberty becomes nothing more than a condition for living as we will, completely free to choose to whom or what we will belong, or simply to possess or exploit. This shallow understanding has little to do with the richness of a liberty directed above all to love.

104. Nor is equality achieved by an abstract proclamation that "all men and women are equal." Instead, it is the result of the conscious and careful cultivation of fraternity. Those capable only of being "associates" create closed worlds. Within that framework, what place is there for those who are not part of one's group of associates, yet long for a better life for themselves and their families?

105. Individualism does not make us more free, more equal, more fraternal. The mere sum of individual interests is not capable of generating a better world for the whole human family. Nor can it save us from the many ills that are now increasingly globalized. Radical individualism is a virus that is extremely difficult to eliminate, for it is clever. It makes us believe that everything consists in giving free rein to our own ambitions, as if by pursuing ever greater ambitions and creating safety nets we would somehow be serving the common good.

A UNIVERSAL LOVE THAT PROMOTES PERSONS

106. Social friendship and universal fraternity necessarily call for an acknowledgement of *the worth of every human person*, always and everywhere. If each individual is of such great worth, it must be stated clearly and firmly that "the mere fact that some people are born in places with fewer resources or less development does not justify the fact that they are living with less dignity."[81] This is a basic principle of social life that

---

[81] Apostolic Exhortation *Evangelii Gaudium* (24 November 2013), 190: AAS 105 (2013), 1100.

tends to be ignored in a variety of ways by those who sense that it does not fit into their worldview or serve their purposes.

107. Every human being has the right to live with dignity and to develop integrally; this fundamental right cannot be denied by any country. People have this right even if they are unproductive, or were born with or developed limitations. This does not detract from their great dignity as human persons, a dignity based not on circumstances but on the intrinsic worth of their being. Unless this basic principle is upheld, there will be no future either for fraternity or for the survival of humanity.

108. Some societies accept this principle in part. They agree that opportunities should be available to everyone, but then go on to say that everything depends on the individual. From this skewed perspective, it would be pointless "to favour an investment in efforts to help the slow, the weak or the less talented to find opportunities in life."[82] Investments in assistance to the vulnerable could prove unprofitable; they might make things less efficient. No. What we need in fact are states and civil institutions that are present and active, that look beyond the free and efficient working of certain economic, political or ideological systems, and are primarily concerned with individuals and the common good.

109. Some people are born into economically stable families, receive a fine education, grow up well nourished, or naturally possess great talent. They will certainly not need a proactive state; they need only claim their freedom. Yet the same rule clearly does not apply to a disabled person, to someone born in dire poverty, to those lacking a good education and with little access to adequate health care. If a society is governed primarily by the criteria of market freedom and efficiency, there is no place for such persons, and fraternity will remain just another vague ideal.

---

[82] Ibid., 209: AAS 105 (2013), 1107.

110. Indeed, "to claim economic freedom while real conditions bar many people from actual access to it, and while possibilities for employment continue to shrink, is to practise doublespeak."[83] Words like freedom, democracy or fraternity prove meaningless, for the fact is that "only when our economic and social system no longer produces even a single victim, a single person cast aside, will we be able to celebrate the feast of universal fraternity."[84] A truly human and fraternal society will be capable of ensuring in an efficient and stable way that each of its members is accompanied at every stage of life. Not only by providing for their basic needs, but by enabling them to give the best of themselves, even though their performance may be less than optimum, their pace slow or their efficiency limited.

111. The human person, with his or her inalienable rights, is by nature open to relationship. Implanted deep within us is the call to transcend ourselves through an encounter with others. For this reason, "care must be taken not to fall into certain errors which can arise from a misunderstanding of the concept of human rights and from its misuse. Today there is a tendency to claim ever broader individual – I am tempted to say individualistic – rights. Underlying this is a conception of the human person as detached from all social and anthropological contexts, as if the person were a "monad" (*monás*), increasingly unconcerned with others... Unless the rights of each individual are harmoniously ordered to the greater good, those rights will end up being considered limitless and consequently will become a source of conflicts and violence."[85]

---

[83] Encyclical Letter *Laudato Si'* (24 May 2015), 129: AAS 107 (2015), 899.

[84] *Message for the "Economy of Francesco" Event* (1 May 2019): *L'Osservatore Romano,* 12 May 2019, 8.

[85] *Address to the European Parliament,* Strasbourg (25 November 2014): AAS 106 (2014), 997.

PROMOTING THE MORAL GOOD

112. Nor can we fail to mention that seeking and pursuing the good of others and of the entire human family also implies helping individuals and societies to mature in the moral values that foster integral human development. The New Testament describes one fruit of the Holy Spirit (cf. *Gal* 5:22) as *agatho-syne*; the Greek word expresses attachment to the good, pursuit of the good. Even more, it suggests a striving for excellence and what is best for others, their growth in maturity and health, the cultivation of values and not simply material wellbeing. A similar expression exists in Latin: *benevolentia*. This is an attitude that "wills the good" of others; it bespeaks a yearning for goodness, an inclination towards all that is fine and excellent, a desire to fill the lives of others with what is beautiful, sublime and edifying.

113. Here, regrettably, I feel bound to reiterate that "we have had enough of immorality and the mockery of ethics, goodness, faith and honesty. It is time to acknowledge that light-hearted superficiality has done us no good. Once the foundations of social life are corroded, what ensues are battles over conflicting interests."[86] Let us return to promoting the good, for ourselves and for the whole human family, and thus advance together towards an authentic and integral growth. Every society needs to ensure that values are passed on; otherwise, what is handed down are selfishness, violence, corruption in its various forms, indifference and, ultimately, a life closed to transcendence and entrenched in individual interests.

The value of solidarity

114. I would like especially to mention solidarity, which, "as a moral virtue and social attitude born of personal conversion,

---

[86] Encyclical Letter *Laudato Si'* (24 May 2015), 229: AAS 107 (2015), 937.

calls for commitment on the part of those responsible for education and formation. I think first of families, called to a primary and vital mission of education. Families are the first place where the values of love and fraternity, togetherness and sharing, concern and care for others are lived out and handed on. They are also the privileged milieu for transmitting the faith, beginning with those first simple gestures of devotion which mothers teach their children. Teachers, who have the challenging task of training children and youth in schools or other settings, should be conscious that their responsibility extends also to the moral, spiritual and social aspects of life. The values of freedom, mutual respect and solidarity can be handed on from a tender age... Communicators also have a responsibility for education and formation, especially nowadays, when the means of information and communication are so widespread."[87]

115. At a time when everything seems to disintegrate and lose consistency, it is good for us to appeal to the "solidity"[88] born of the consciousness that we are responsible for the fragility of others as we strive to build a common future. Solidarity finds concrete expression in service, which can take a variety of forms in an effort to care for others. And service in great part means "caring for vulnerability, for the vulnerable members of our families, our society, our people." In offering such service, individuals learn to "set aside their own wishes and desires, their pursuit of power, before the concrete gaze of those who are most vulnerable... Service always looks to their faces, touches their flesh, senses their closeness and even, in some cases, 'suffers' that closeness and tries to help them. Service is never ideological, for we do not serve ideas, we serve people."[89]

---

[87] *Message for the 2016 World Day of Peace* (8 December 2015), 6: AAS 108 (2016), 57-58.

[88] Solidity is etymologically related to "solidarity." Solidarity, in the ethical-political meaning that it has taken on in the last two centuries, results in a secure and firm social compact.

[89] *Homily*, Havana, Cuba (20 September 2015): *L'Osservatore Romano*, 21-22 September 2015, 8.

116. The needy generally "practise the special solidarity that exists among those who are poor and suffering, and which our civilization seems to have forgotten or would prefer in fact to forget. Solidarity is a word that is not always well received; in certain situations, it has become a dirty word, a word that dare not be said. Solidarity means much more than engaging in sporadic acts of generosity. It means thinking and acting in terms of community. It means that the lives of all are prior to the appropriation of goods by a few. It also means combatting the structural causes of poverty, inequality, the lack of work, land and housing, the denial of social and labour rights. It means confronting the destructive effects of the empire of money… Solidarity, understood in its most profound meaning, is a way of making history, and this is what popular movements are doing."[90]

117. When we speak of the need to care for our common home, our planet, we appeal to that spark of universal consciousness and mutual concern that may still be present in people's hearts. Those who enjoy a surplus of water yet choose to conserve it for the sake of the greater human family have attained a moral stature that allows them to look beyond themselves and the group to which they belong. How marvellously human! The same attitude is demanded if we are to recognize the rights of all people, even those born beyond our own borders.

RE-ENVISAGING THE SOCIAL ROLE OF PROPERTY

118. The world exists for everyone, because all of us were born with the same dignity. Differences of colour, religion, talent, place of birth or residence, and so many others, cannot be used to justify the privileges of some over the rights of all. As a community, we have an obligation to ensure that every person

---

[90] *Address to Participants in the Meeting of Popular Movements* (28 October 2014): AAS 106 (2014), 851-852.

lives with dignity and has sufficient opportunities for his or her integral development.

119. In the first Christian centuries, a number of thinkers developed a universal vision in their reflections on the common destination of created goods.[91] This led them to realize that if one person lacks what is necessary to live with dignity, it is because another person is detaining it. Saint John Chrysostom summarizes it in this way: "Not to share our wealth with the poor is to rob them and take away their livelihood. The riches we possess are not our own, but theirs as well."[92] In the words of Saint Gregory the Great, "When we provide the needy with their basic needs, we are giving them what belongs to them, not to us."[93]

120. Once more, I would like to echo a statement of Saint John Paul II whose forcefulness has perhaps been insufficiently recognized: "God gave the earth to the whole human race for the sustenance of all its members, without excluding or favouring anyone."[94] For my part, I would observe that "the Christian tradition has never recognized the right to private property as absolute or inviolable, and has stressed the social purpose of all forms of private property."[95] The principle of the common use of created goods is the "first principle of the whole ethical and social order";[96] it is a natural and inherent right that

---

[91] Cf. Saint Basil, *Homilia XXI, Quod rebus mundanis adhaerendum non sit*, 3.5: PG 31, 545-549; *Regulae brevius tractatae*, 92: PG 31, 1145-1148; Saint peter chrysologus, *Sermo* 123: PL 52, 536-540; Saint Ambrose, *De Nabuthe*, 27.52: PL 14, 738ff.; Saint Augustine, *In Iohannis Evangelium*, 6, 25: PL 35, 1436ff.

[92] *De Lazaro Concio*, II, 6: PG 48, 992D.

[93] *Regula Pastoralis*, III, 21: PL 77, 87.

[94] Saint John Paul II, Encyclical Letter *Centesimus Annus* (1 May 1991), 31: AAS 83 (1991), 831.

[95] Encyclical Letter *Laudato Si'* (24 May 2015), 93: AAS 107 (2015), 884.

[96] Saint John Paul II, Encyclical Letter *Laborem Exercens* (14 September 1981), 19: AAS 73 (1981), 626.

takes priority over others.[97] All other rights having to do with the goods necessary for the integral fulfilment of persons, including that of private property or any other type of property, should – in the words of Saint Paul VI – "in no way hinder , but should actively facilitate its implementation."[98] The right to private property can only be considered a secondary natural right, derived from the principle of the universal destination of created goods. This has concrete consequences that ought to be reflected in the workings of society. Yet it often happens that secondary rights displace primary and overriding rights, in practice making them irrelevant.

Rights without borders

121. No one, then, can remain excluded because of his or her place of birth, much less because of privileges enjoyed by others who were born in lands of greater opportunity. The limits and borders of individual states cannot stand in the way of this. As it is unacceptable that some have fewer rights by virtue of being women, it is likewise unacceptable that the mere place of one's birth or residence should result in his or her possessing fewer opportunities for a developed and dignified life.

122. Development must not aim at the amassing of wealth by a few, but must ensure "human rights – personal and social, economic and political, including the rights of nations and of peoples."[99] The right of some to free enterprise or market freedom cannot supersede the rights of peoples and the dignity of the poor, or, for that matter, respect for the natural environment,

---

[97] Cf.Pontifical Council for Justice and Peace, *Compendium of the Social Doctrine of the Church*, 172.

[98] Encyclical Letter *Populorum Progressio* (26 March 1967): AAS 59 (1967), 268.

[99] Saint John Paul II, Encyclical Letter *Sollicitudo Rei Socialis* (30 December 1987), 33: AAS 80 (1988), 557.

for "if we make something our own, it is only to administer it for the good of all."[100]

123. Business activity is essentially "a noble vocation, directed to producing wealth and improving our world."[101] God encourages us to develop the talents he gave us, and he has made our universe one of immense potential. In God's plan, each individual is called to promote his or her own development,[102] and this includes finding the best economic and technological means of multiplying goods and increasing wealth. Business abilities, which are a gift from God, should always be clearly directed to the development of others and to eliminating poverty, especially through the creation of diversified work opportunities. The right to private property is always accompanied by the primary and prior principle of the subordination of all private property to the universal destination of the earth's goods, and thus the right of all to their use.[103]

The rights of peoples

124. Nowadays, a firm belief in the common destination of the earth's goods requires that this principle also be applied to nations, their territories and their resources. Seen from the standpoint not only of the legitimacy of private property and the rights of its citizens, but also of the first principle of the common destination of goods, we can then say that each country also belongs to the foreigner, inasmuch as a territory's goods must not be denied to a needy person coming from elsewhere.

---

[100] Encyclical Letter *Laudato Si'* (24 May 2015), 95: AAS 107 (2015), 885.

[101] Ibid., 129: AAS 107 (2015), 899.

[102] Cf. Saint Paul VI, Encyclical Letter *Populorum Progressio* (26 March 1967): AAS 59 (1967), 265; Benedict XVI, Encyclical Letter *Caritas in Veritate* (29 June 2009), 16: AAS 101 (2009), 652

[103] Cf. Encyclical Letter *Laudato Si'* (24 May 2015), 93: AAS 107 (2015), 884-885; Apostolic Exhortation *Evangelii Gaudium* (24 November 2013), 189-190: AAS 105 (2013), 1099-1100.

As the Bishops of the United States have taught, there are fundamental rights that "precede any society because they flow from the dignity granted to each person as created by God."[104]

125. This presupposes a different way of understanding relations and exchanges between countries. If every human being possesses an inalienable dignity, if all people are my brothers and sisters, and if the world truly belongs to everyone, then it matters little whether my neighbour was born in my country or elsewhere. My own country also shares responsibility for his or her development, although it can fulfil that responsibility in a variety of ways. It can offer a generous welcome to those in urgent need, or work to improve living conditions in their native lands by refusing to exploit those countries or to drain them of natural resources, backing corrupt systems that hinder the dignified development of their peoples. What applies to nations is true also for different regions within each country, since there too great inequalities often exist. At times, the inability to recognize equal human dignity leads the more developed regions in some countries to think that they can jettison the "dead weight" of poorer regions and so increase their level of consumption.

126. We are really speaking about a new network of international relations, since there is no way to resolve the serious problems of our world if we continue to think only in terms of mutual assistance between individuals or small groups. Nor should we forget that "inequity affects not only individuals but entire countries; it compels us to consider an ethics of international relations."[105] Indeed, justice requires recognizing and respecting not only the rights of individuals, but also social

---

[104] United States Conference of Catholic Bishops, Pastoral Letter Against Racism *Open Wide Our Hearts: The Enduring Call to Love* (November 2018).

[105] Encyclical Letter *Laudato Si'* (24 May 2015), 51: AAS 107 (2015), 867.

rights and the rights of peoples.[106] This means finding a way to ensure "the fundamental right of peoples to subsistence and progress,"[107] a right which is at times severely restricted by the pressure created by foreign debt. In many instances, debt repayment not only fails to promote development but gravely limits and conditions it. While respecting the principle that all legitimately acquired debt must be repaid, the way in which many poor countries fulfil this obligation should not end up compromising their very existence and growth.

127. Certainly, all this calls for an alternative way of thinking. Without an attempt to enter into that way of thinking, what I am saying here will sound wildly unrealistic. On the other hand, if we accept the great principle that there are rights born of our inalienable human dignity, we can rise to the challenge of envisaging a new humanity. We can aspire to a world that provides land, housing and work for all. This is the true path of peace, not the senseless and myopic strategy of sowing fear and mistrust in the face of outside threats. For a real and lasting peace will only be possible "on the basis of a global ethic of solidarity and cooperation in the service of a future shaped by interdependence and shared responsibility in the whole human family."[108]

CHAPTER FOUR

A HEART OPEN TO THE WHOLE WORLD

128. If the conviction that all human beings are brothers and sisters is not to remain an abstract idea but to find concrete

---

[106] Cf. Benedict XVI, Encyclical Letter *Caritas in Veritate* (29 June 2009), 6: AAS 101 (2009), 644.

[107] Saint John Paul II, Encyclical Letter *Centesimus Annus* (1 May 1991), 35: AAS 83 (1991), 838.

[108] *Address on Nuclear Weapons,* Nagasaki, Japan (24 November 2019): *L'Osservatore Romano,* 25-26 November 2019, 6.

embodiment, then numerous related issues emerge, forcing us to see things in a new light and to develop new responses.

BORDERS AND THEIR LIMITS

129. Complex challenges arise when our neighbour happens to be an immigrant.[109] Ideally, unnecessary migration ought to be avoided; this entails creating in countries of origin the conditions needed for a dignified life and integral development. Yet until substantial progress is made in achieving this goal, we are obliged to respect the right of all individuals to find a place that meets their basic needs and those of their families, and where they can find personal fulfilment. Our response to the arrival of migrating persons can be summarized by four words: welcome, protect, promote and integrate. For "it is not a case of implementing welfare programmes from the top down, but rather of undertaking a journey together, through these four actions, in order to build cities and countries that, while preserving their respective cultural and religious identity, are open to differences and know how to promote them in the spirit of human fraternity."[110]

130. This implies taking certain indispensable steps, especially in response to those who are fleeing grave humanitarian crises. As examples, we may cite: increasing and simplifying the granting of visas; adopting programmes of individual and community sponsorship; opening humanitarian corridors for the most vulnerable refugees; providing suitable and dignified housing; guaranteeing personal security and access to basic services; ensuring adequate consular assistance and the right to retain personal identity documents; equitable access to the

---

[109] Cf. CATHOLIC BISHOPS OF MEXICO AND THE UNITED STATES, *A Pastoral Letter Concerning Migration: "Strangers No Longer Together on the Journey of Hope"* (January 2003).

[110] *General Audience* (3 April 2019): *L'Osservatore Romano*, 4 April 2019, p. 8.

justice system; the possibility of opening bank accounts and the guarantee of the minimum needed to survive; freedom of movement and the possibility of employment; protecting minors and ensuring their regular access to education; providing for programmes of temporary guardianship or shelter; guaranteeing religious freedom; promoting integration into society; supporting the reuniting of families; and preparing local communities for the process of integration.[111]

131. For those who are not recent arrivals and already participate in the fabric of society, it is important to apply the concept of "citizenship," which "is based on the equality of rights and duties, under which all enjoy justice. It is therefore crucial to establish in our societies the concept of *full citizenship* and to reject the discriminatory use of the term *minorities*, which engenders feelings of isolation and inferiority. Its misuse paves the way for hostility and discord; it undoes any successes and takes away the religious and civil rights of some citizens who are thus discriminated against."[112]

132. Even when they take such essential steps, states are not able, on their own, to implement adequate solutions, "since the consequences of the decisions made by each inevitably have repercussions on the entire international community." As a result, "our response can only be the fruit of a common effort"[113] to develop a form of global governance with regard to movements of migration. Thus, there is "a need for mid-term and long-term planning which is not limited to emergency responses. Such planning should include effective assistance for integrating migrants in their receiving countries, while also promoting

---

[111] Cf. *Message for the 2018 World Day of Migrants and Refugees* (14 January 2018): AAS 109 (2017), 918-923.

[112] *Document on Human Fraternity for World Peace and Living Together*, Abu Dhabi (4 February 2019): *L'Osservatore Romano*, 4-5 February 2019, p. 7.

[113] *Address to the Diplomatic Corps Accredited to the Holy See*, 11 January 2016: AAS 108 (2016), 124.

the development of their countries of origin through policies inspired by solidarity, yet not linking assistance to ideological strategies and practices alien or contrary to the cultures of the peoples being assisted."[114]

RECIPROCAL GIFTS

133. The arrival of those who are different, coming from other ways of life and cultures, can be a gift, for "the stories of migrants are always stories of an encounter between individuals and between cultures. For the communities and societies to which they come, migrants bring an opportunity for enrichment and the integral human development of all."[115] For this reason, "I especially urge young people not to play into the hands of those who would set them against other young people, newly arrived in their countries, and who would encourage them to view the latter as a threat, and not possessed of the same inalienable dignity as every other human being."[116]

134. Indeed, when we open our hearts to those who are different, this enables them, while continuing to be themselves, to develop in new ways. The different cultures that have flourished over the centuries need to be preserved, lest our world be impoverished. At the same time, those cultures should be encouraged to be open to new experiences through their encounter with other realities, for the risk of succumbing to cultural sclerosis is always present. That is why "we need to communicate with each other, to discover the gifts of each person, to promote that which unites us, and to regard our differences as an opportunity to grow in mutual respect. Patience and trust are called for in such dialogue, permitting individuals, families

---

[114] Ibid., 122.
[115] Post-Synodal Apostolic Exhortation *Christus Vivit* (25 March 2019), 93.
[116] Ibid., 94.

and communities to hand on the values of their own culture and welcome the good that comes from others' experiences."[117]

135. Here I would mention some examples that I have used in the past. Latino culture is "a ferment of values and possibilities that can greatly enrich the United States," for "intense immigration always ends up influencing and transforming the culture of a place… In Argentina, intense immigration from Italy has left a mark on the culture of the society, and the presence of some 200,000 Jews has a great effect on the cultural 'style' of Buenos Aires. Immigrants, if they are helped to integrate, are a blessing, a source of enrichment and new gift that encourages a society to grow."[118]

136. On an even broader scale, Grand Imam Ahmad Al-Tayyeb and I have observed that "good relations between East and West are indisputably necessary for both. They must not be neglected, so that each can be enriched by the other's culture through fruitful exchange and dialogue. The West can discover in the East remedies for those spiritual and religious maladies that are caused by a prevailing materialism. And the East can find in the West many elements that can help free it from weakness, division, conflict and scientific, technical and cultural decline. It is important to pay attention to religious, cultural and historical differences that are a vital component in shaping the character, culture and civilization of the East. It is likewise important to reinforce the bond of fundamental human rights in order to help ensure a dignified life for all the men and women of East and West, avoiding the politics of double standards."[119]

---

[117] *Address to Authorities*, Sarajevo, Bosnia and Herzegovina (6 June 2015): *L'Osservatore Romano*, 7 June 2015, p. 7.

[118] *Latinoamérica. Conversaciones con Hernán Reyes Alcaide*, ed. Planeta, Buenos Aires, 2017, 105.

[119] *Document on Human Fraternity for World Peace and Living Together*, Abu Dhabi (4 February 2019): *L'Osservatore Romano*, 4-5 February 2019, p. 7

A fruitful exchange

137. Mutual assistance between countries proves enriching for each. A country that moves forward while remaining solidly grounded in its original cultural substratum is a treasure for the whole of humanity. We need to develop the awareness that nowadays we are either all saved together or no one is saved. Poverty, decadence and suffering in one part of the earth are a silent breeding ground for problems that will end up affecting the entire planet. If we are troubled by the extinction of certain species, we should be all the more troubled that in some parts of our world individuals or peoples are prevented from developing their potential and beauty by poverty or other structural limitations. In the end, this will impoverish us all.

138. Although this has always been true, never has it been more evident than in our own day, when the world is interconnected by globalization. We need to attain a global juridical, political and economic order "which can increase and give direction to international cooperation for the development of all peoples in solidarity."[120] Ultimately, this will benefit the entire world, since "development aid for poor countries" implies "creating wealth for all."[121] From the standpoint of integral development, this presupposes "giving poorer nations an effective voice in shared decision-making"[122] and the capacity to "facilitate access to the international market on the part of countries suffering from poverty and underdevelopment."[123]

A gratuitousness open to others

139. Even so, I do not wish to limit this presentation to a kind of utilitarian approach. There is always the factor of "gratuitous-

---

[120] BENEDICT XVI, Encyclical Letter *Caritas in Veritate* (29 June 2009), 67: AAS 101 (2009), 700.
[121] Ibid., 60: AAS 101 (2009), 695.
[122] Ibid., 67: AAS 101 (2009), 700
[123] PONTIFICAL COUNCIL FOR JUSTICE AND PEACE, *Compendium of the Social Doctrine of the Church*, 447.

ness": the ability to do some things simply because they are good in themselves, without concern for personal gain or recompense. Gratuitousness makes it possible for us to welcome the stranger, even though this brings us no immediate tangible benefit. Some countries, though, presume to accept only scientists or investors.

140. Life without fraternal gratuitousness becomes a form of frenetic commerce, in which we are constantly weighing up what we give and what we get back in return. God, on the other hand, gives freely, to the point of helping even those who are unfaithful; he "makes his sun rise on the evil and on the good" (*Mt* 5:45). There is a reason why Jesus told us: "When you give alms, do not let your right hand know what your left hand is doing, so that your alms may be in secret" (*Mt* 6:3-4). We received life freely; we paid nothing for it. Consequently, all of us are able to give without expecting anything in return, to do good to others without demanding that they treat us well in return. As Jesus told his disciples: "Without cost you have received, without cost you are to give" (*Mt* 10:8).

141. The true worth of the different countries of our world is measured by their ability to think not simply as a country but also as part of the larger human family. This is seen especially in times of crisis. Narrow forms of nationalism are an extreme expression of an inability to grasp the meaning of this gratuitousness. They err in thinking that they can develop on their own, heedless of the ruin of others, that by closing their doors to others they will be better protected. Immigrants are seen as usurpers who have nothing to offer. This leads to the simplistic belief that the poor are dangerous and useless, while the powerful are generous benefactors. Only a social and political culture that readily and "gratuitously" welcomes others will have a future.

LOCAL AND UNIVERSAL

142. It should be kept in mind that "an innate tension exists between globalization and localization. We need to pay attention

to the global so as to avoid narrowness and banality. Yet we also need to look to the local, which keeps our feet on the ground. Together, the two prevent us from falling into one of two extremes. In the first, people get caught up in an abstract, globalized universe... In the other, they turn into a museum of local folklore, a world apart, doomed to doing the same things over and over, incapable of being challenged by novelty or appreciating the beauty which God bestows beyond their borders."[124] We need to have a global outlook to save ourselves from petty provincialism. When our house stops being a home and starts to become an enclosure, a cell, then the global comes to our rescue, like a "final cause" that draws us towards our fulfilment. At the same time, though, the local has to be eagerly embraced, for it possesses something that the global does not: it is capable of being a leaven, of bringing enrichment, of sparking mechanisms of subsidiarity. Universal fraternity and social friendship are thus two inseparable and equally vital poles in every society. To separate them would be to disfigure each and to create a dangerous polarization.

Local flavour

143. The solution is not an openness that spurns its own richness. Just as there can be no dialogue with "others" without a sense of our own identity, so there can be no openness between peoples except on the basis of love for one's own land, one's own people, one's own cultural roots. I cannot truly encounter another unless I stand on firm foundations, for it is on the basis of these that I can accept the gift the other brings and in turn offer an authentic gift of my own. I can welcome others who are different, and value the unique contribution they have to make, only if I am firmly rooted in my own people and culture. Everyone loves and cares for his or her native land and village, just as they love and care for

---

[124] Apostolic Exhortation *Evangelii Gaudium* (24 November 2013), 234: AAS 105 (2013), 1115

their home and are personally responsible for its upkeep. The common good likewise requires that we protect and love our native land. Otherwise, the consequences of a disaster in one country will end up affecting the entire planet. All this brings out the positive meaning of the right to property: I care for and cultivate something that I possess, in such a way that it can contribute to the good of all.

144. It also gives rise to healthy and enriching exchanges. The experience of being raised in a particular place and sharing in a particular culture gives us insight into aspects of reality that others cannot so easily perceive. Universal does not necessarily mean bland, uniform and standardized, based on a single prevailing cultural model, for this will ultimately lead to the loss of a rich palette of shades and colours, and result in utter monotony. Such was the temptation referred to in the ancient account of the Tower of Babel. The attempt to build a tower that would reach to heaven was not an expression of unity between various peoples speaking to one another from their diversity. Instead, it was a misguided attempt, born of pride and ambition, to create a unity other than that willed by God in his providential plan for the nations (cf. *Gen* 11:1-9).

145. There can be a false openness to the universal, born of the shallowness of those lacking insight into the genius of their native land or harbouring unresolved resentment towards their own people. Whatever the case, "we constantly have to broaden our horizons and see the greater good which will benefit us all. But this has to be done without evasion or uprooting. We need to sink our roots deeper into the fertile soil and history of our native place, which is a gift of God. We can work on a small scale, in our own neighbourhood, but with a larger perspective... The global need not stifle, nor the particular prove barren";[125] our model must be that of a polyhedron, in which the value of each individual is respected, where "the whole is

---

[125] Ibid., 235: AAS 105 (2013), 1115.

greater than the part, but it is also greater than the sum of its parts."[126]

A universal horizon

146. There is a kind of "local" narcissism unrelated to a healthy love of one's own people and culture. It is born of a certain insecurity and fear of the other that leads to rejection and the desire to erect walls for self-defence. Yet it is impossible to be "local" in a healthy way without being sincerely open to the universal, without feeling challenged by what is happening in other places, without openness to enrichment by other cultures, and without solidarity and concern for the tragedies affecting other peoples. A "local narcissism" instead frets over a limited number of ideas, customs and forms of security; incapable of admiring the vast potential and beauty offered by the larger world, it lacks an authentic and generous spirit of solidarity. Life on the local level thus becomes less and less welcoming, people less open to complementarity. Its possibilities for development narrow; it grows weary and infirm. A healthy culture, on the other hand, is open and welcoming by its very nature; indeed, "a culture without universal values is not truly a culture."[127]

147. Let us realize that as our minds and hearts narrow, the less capable we become of understanding the world around us. Without encountering and relating to differences, it is hard to achieve a clear and complete understanding even of ourselves and of our native land. Other cultures are not "enemies" from which we need to protect ourselves, but differing reflections of the inexhaustible richness of human life. Seeing ourselves from

---

[126] Ibid.

[127] SAINT JOHN PAUL II, *Address to Representatives of Argentinian Culture*, Buenos Aires, Argentina (12 April 1987), 4: *L'Osservatore Romano*, 14 April 1987, p. 7.

the perspective of another, of one who is different, we can better recognize our own unique features and those of our culture: its richness, its possibilities and its limitations. Our local experience needs to develop "in contrast to" and "in harmony with" the experiences of others living in diverse cultural contexts.[128]

148. In fact, a healthy openness never threatens one's own identity. A living culture, enriched by elements from other places, does not import a mere carbon copy of those new elements, but integrates them in its own unique way. The result is a new synthesis that is ultimately beneficial to all, since the original culture itself ends up being nourished. That is why I have urged indigenous peoples to cherish their roots and their ancestral cultures. At the same time, though, I have wanted to stress that I have no intention of proposing "a completely enclosed, a-historic, static 'indigenism' that would reject any kind of blending (*mestizaje*)." For "our own cultural identity is strengthened and enriched as a result of dialogue with those unlike ourselves. Nor is our authentic identity preserved by an impoverished isolation."[129] The world grows and is filled with new beauty, thanks to the successive syntheses produced between cultures that are open and free of any form of cultural imposition.

149. For a healthy relationship between love of one's native land and a sound sense of belonging to our larger human family, it is helpful to keep in mind that global society is not the sum total of different countries, but rather the communion that exists among them. The mutual sense of belonging is prior to the emergence of individual groups. Each particular group becomes part of the fabric of universal communion and there discovers its own beauty. All individuals, whatever their origin, know that

---

[128] Cf. ID., *Address to the Roman Curia* (21 December 1984), 4: AAS 76 (1984), 506.

[129] Post-Synodal Apostolic Exhortation *Querida Amazonia* (2 February 2020), 37.

they are part of the greater human family, without which they will not be able to understand themselves fully.

150. To see things in this way brings the joyful realization that no one people, culture or individual can achieve everything on its own: to attain fulfilment in life we need others. An awareness of our own limitations and incompleteness, far from being a threat, becomes the key to envisaging and pursuing a common project. For "man is a limited being who is himself limitless."[130]

Starting with our own region

151. Thanks to regional exchanges, by which poorer countries become open to the wider world, universality does not necessarily water down their distinct features. An appropriate and authentic openness to the world presupposes the capacity to be open to one's neighbour within a family of nations. Cultural, economic and political integration with neighbouring peoples should therefore be accompanied by a process of education that promotes the value of love for one's neighbour, the first indispensable step towards attaining a healthy universal integration.

152. In some areas of our cities, there is still a lively sense of neighbourhood. Each person quite spontaneously perceives a duty to accompany and help his or her neighbour. In places where these community values are maintained, people experience a closeness marked by gratitude, solidarity and reciprocity. The neighbourhood gives them a sense of shared identity.[131] Would that neighbouring countries were able to

---

[130] GEORG SIMMEL, *Brücke und Tür. Essays des Philosophen zur Geschichte, Religion, Kunst und Gesellschaft*, ed. Michael Landmann, Köhler-Verlag, Stuttgart, 1957, 6.
[131] Cf. JAIME HOYOS-VÁSQUEZ, S.J., "Lógica de las relaciones sociales. Reflexión onto-lógica," *Revista Universitas Philosophica*, 15-16 (December 1990-June 1991), Bogotá, 95-106

encourage a similar neighbourly spirit between their peoples! Yet the spirit of individualism also affects relations between countries. The danger of thinking that we have to protect ourselves from one another, of viewing others as competitors or dangerous enemies, also affects relations between peoples in the same region. Perhaps we were trained in this kind of fear and mistrust.

153. There are powerful countries and large businesses that profit from this isolation and prefer to negotiate with each country separately. On the other hand, small or poor countries can sign agreements with their regional neighbours that will allow them to negotiate as a bloc and thus avoid being cut off, isolated and dependent on the great powers. Today, no state can ensure the common good of its population if it remains isolated.

CHAPTER FIVE

A BETTER KIND OF POLITICS

154. The development of a global community of fraternity based on the practice of social friendship on the part of peoples and nations calls for a better kind of politics, one truly at the service of the common good. Sadly, politics today often takes forms that hinder progress towards a different world.

FORMS OF POPULISM AND LIBERALISM

155. Lack of concern for the vulnerable can hide behind a populism that exploits them demagogically for its own purposes, or a liberalism that serves the economic interests of the powerful. In both cases, it becomes difficult to envisage an open world that makes room for everyone, including the most vulnerable, and shows respect for different cultures.

Popular vs. populist

156. In recent years, the words "populism" and "populist" have invaded the communications media and everyday conversation. As a result, they have lost whatever value they might have had, and have become another source of polarization in an already divided society. Efforts are made to classify entire peoples, groups, societies and governments as "populist" or not. Nowadays it has become impossible for someone to express a view on any subject without being categorized one way or the other, either to be unfairly discredited or to be praised to the skies.

157. The attempt to see populism as a key for interpreting social reality is problematic in another way: it disregards the legitimate meaning of the word "people." Any effort to remove this concept from common parlance could lead to the elimination of the very notion of democracy as "government by the people." If we wish to maintain that society is more than a mere aggregate of individuals, the term "people" proves necessary. There are social phenomena that create majorities, as well as megatrends and communitarian aspirations. Men and women are capable of coming up with shared goals that transcend their differences and can thus engage in a common endeavour. Then too, it is extremely difficult to carry out a long-term project unless it becomes a collective aspiration. All these factors lie behind our use of the words "people" and "popular." Unless they are taken into account – together with a sound critique of demagoguery – a fundamental aspect of social reality would be overlooked.

158. Here, there can be a misunderstanding. "'People' is not a logical category, nor is it a mystical category, if by that we mean that everything the people does is good, or that the people is an 'angelic' reality. Rather, it is a mythic category... When you have to explain what you mean by people, you use logical categories for the sake of explanation, and necessarily so. Yet in that way you cannot explain what it means to belong to a people. The word 'people' has a deeper meaning that cannot

be set forth in purely logical terms. To be part of a people is to be part of a shared identity arising from social and cultural bonds. And that is not something automatic, but rather a slow, difficult process... of advancing towards a common project."[132]

159. "Popular" leaders, those capable of interpreting the feelings and cultural dynamics of a people, and significant trends in society, do exist. The service they provide by their efforts to unite and lead can become the basis of an enduring vision of transformation and growth that would also include making room for others in the pursuit of the common good. But this can degenerate into an unhealthy "populism" when individuals are able to exploit politically a people's culture, under whatever ideological banner, for their own personal advantage or continuing grip on power. Or when, at other times, they seek popularity by appealing to the basest and most selfish inclinations of certain sectors of the population. This becomes all the more serious when, whether in cruder or more subtle forms, it leads to the usurpation of institutions and laws.

160. Closed populist groups distort the word "people," since they are not talking about a true people. The concept of "people" is in fact open-ended. A living and dynamic people, a people with a future, is one constantly open to a new synthesis through its ability to welcome differences. In this way, it does not deny its proper identity, but is open to being mobilized, challenged, broadened and enriched by others, and thus to further growth and development.

161. Another sign of the decline of popular leadership is concern for short-term advantage. One meets popular demands

---

[132] ANTONIO SPADARO, S.J., *Le orme di un pastore. Una conversazione con Papa Francesco,* in JORGE MARIO BERGOLIO – PAPA FRANCESCO, *Nei tuoi occhi è la mia parola. Omelie e discorsi di Buenos Aires 1999-2013,* Rizzoli, Milan 2016, XVI; cf. Apostolic Exhortation *Evangelii Gaudium* (24 November 2013), 220-221: AAS 105 (2013), 1110-1111.

for the sake of gaining votes or support, but without advancing in an arduous and constant effort to generate the resources people need to develop and earn a living by their own efforts and creativity. In this regard, I have made it clear that "I have no intention of proposing an irresponsible populism."[133] Eliminating inequality requires an economic growth that can help to tap each region's potential and thus guarantee a sustainable equality.[134] At the same time, it follows that "welfare projects, which meet certain urgent needs, should be considered merely temporary responses."[135]

162. The biggest issue is employment. The truly "popular" thing – since it promotes the good of the people – is to provide everyone with the opportunity to nurture the seeds that God has planted in each of us: our talents, our initiative and our innate resources. This is the finest help we can give to the poor, the best path to a life of dignity. Hence my insistence that, "helping the poor financially must always be a provisional solution in the face of pressing needs. The broader objective should always be to allow them a dignified life through work."[136] Since production systems may change, political systems must keep working to structure society in such a way that everyone has a chance to contribute his or her own talents and efforts. For "there is no poverty worse than that which takes away work and the dignity of work."[137] In a genuinely developed society, work is an essential dimension of social life, for it is not only a means of earning one's daily bread, but also of personal growth, the

---

[133] Apostolic Exaltation *Evangelii Gaudium* (24 November 2013), 204: AAS 105 (2013), 1106.

[134] Cf. ibid.: AAS 105 (2013), 1105-1106.

[135] Ibid., 202: AAS 105 (2013), 1105.

[136] Encyclical Letter *Laudato Si'* (24 May 2015), 128: AAS 107 (2015), 898.

[137] *Address to the Diplomatic Corps Accredited to the Holy See* (12 January 2015): AAS 107 (2015), 165; cf. *Address to Participants in the World Meeting of Popular Movements* (28 October 2014): AAS 106 (2014), 851-859.

building of healthy relationships, self-expression and the exchange of gifts. Work gives us a sense of shared responsibility for the development of the world, and ultimately, for our life as a people.

The benefits and limits of liberal approaches

163. The concept of a "people," which naturally entails a positive view of community and cultural bonds, is usually rejected by individualistic liberal approaches, which view society as merely the sum of coexisting interests. One speaks of respect for freedom, but without roots in a shared narrative; in certain contexts, those who defend the rights of the most vulnerable members of society tend to be criticized as populists. The notion of a people is considered an abstract construct, something that does not really exist. But this is to create a needless dichotomy. Neither the notion of "people" nor that of "neighbour" can be considered purely abstract or romantic, in such a way that social organization, science and civic institutions can be rejected or treated with contempt.[138]

164. Charity, on the other hand, unites both dimensions – the abstract and the institutional – since it calls for an effective process of historical change that embraces everything: institutions, law, technology, experience, professional expertise, scientific analysis, administrative procedures, and so forth. For that matter, "private life cannot exist unless it is protected by public order. A domestic hearth has no real warmth unless it is safeguarded by law, by a state of tranquillity founded on law, and enjoys a minimum of wellbeing ensured by the division of labour, commercial exchange, social justice and political citizenship."[139]

---

[138] A similar point could be made with regard to the biblical category of the Kingdom of God.

[139] PAUL RICOEUR, *Histoire et Verité*, ed. Le Seuil Paris, 1967, 122.

165. True charity is capable of incorporating all these elements in its concern for others. In the case of personal encounters, including those involving a distant or forgotten brother or sister, it can do so by employing all the resources that the institutions of an organized, free and creative society are capable of generating. Even the Good Samaritan, for example, needed to have a nearby inn that could provide the help that he was personally unable to offer. Love of neighbour is concrete and squanders none of the resources needed to bring about historical change that can benefit the poor and disadvantaged. At times, however, leftist ideologies or social doctrines linked to individualistic ways of acting and ineffective procedures affect only a few, while the majority of those left behind remain dependent on the goodwill of others. This demonstrates the need for a greater spirit of fraternity, but also a more efficient worldwide organization to help resolve the problems plaguing the abandoned who are suffering and dying in poor countries. It also shows that there is no one solution, no single acceptable methodology, no economic recipe that can be applied indiscriminately to all. Even the most rigorous scientific studies can propose different courses of action.

166. Everything, then, depends on our ability to see the need for a change of heart, attitudes and lifestyles. Otherwise, political propaganda, the media and the shapers of public opinion will continue to promote an individualistic and uncritical culture subservient to unregulated economic interests and societal institutions at the service of those who already enjoy too much power. My criticism of the technocratic paradigm involves more than simply thinking that if we control its excesses everything will be fine. The bigger risk does not come from specific objects, material realities or institutions, but from the way that they are used. It has to do with human weakness, the proclivity to selfishness that is part of what the Christian tradition refers to as "concupiscence": the human inclination to be concerned only with myself, my group, my own petty interests. Concupiscence is not a flaw limited to our own day. It has been present from

the beginning of humanity, and has simply changed and taken on different forms down the ages, using whatever means each moment of history can provide. Concupiscence, however, can be overcome with the help of God.

167. Education and upbringing, concern for others, a well-integrated view of life and spiritual growth: all these are essential for quality human relationships and for enabling society itself to react against injustices, aberrations and abuses of economic, technological, political and media power. Some liberal approaches ignore this factor of human weakness; they envisage a world that follows a determined order and is capable by itself of ensuring a bright future and providing solutions for every problem.

168. The marketplace, by itself, cannot resolve every problem, however much we are asked to believe this dogma of neoliberal faith. Whatever the challenge, this impoverished and repetitive school of thought always offers the same recipes. Neoliberalism simply reproduces itself by resorting to the magic theories of "spillover" or "trickle" – without using the name – as the only solution to societal problems. There is little appreciation of the fact that the alleged "spillover" does not resolve the inequality that gives rise to new forms of violence threatening the fabric of society. It is imperative to have a proactive economic policy directed at "promoting an economy that favours productive diversity and business creativity"[140] and makes it possible for jobs to be created and not cut. Financial speculation fundamentally aimed at quick profit continues to wreak havoc. Indeed, "without internal forms of solidarity and mutual trust, the market cannot completely fulfil its proper economic function. And today this trust has ceased to exist."[141] The story did not end the

---

[140] Encyclical Letter *Laudato Si'* (24 May 2015), 129: AAS 107 (2015), 899.

[141] BENEDICT XVI, Encyclical Letter *Caritas in Veritate* (29 June 2009), 35: AAS 101 (2009), 670.

way it was meant to, and the dogmatic formulae of prevailing economic theory proved not to be infallible. The fragility of world systems in the face of the pandemic has demonstrated that not everything can be resolved by market freedom. It has also shown that, in addition to recovering a sound political life that is not subject to the dictates of finance, "we must put human dignity back at the centre and on that pillar build the alternative social structures we need."[142]

169. In some closed and monochrome economic approaches, for example, there seems to be no place for popular movements that unite the unemployed, temporary and informal workers and many others who do not easily find a place in existing structures. Yet those movements manage various forms of popular economy and of community production. What is needed is a model of social, political and economic participation "that can include popular movements and invigorate local, national and international governing structures with that torrent of moral energy that springs from including the excluded in the building of a common destiny," while also ensuring that "these experiences of solidarity which grow up from below, from the subsoil of the planet – can come together, be more coordinated, keep on meeting one another."[143] This, however, must happen in a way that will not betray their distinctive way of acting as "sowers of change, promoters of a process involving millions of actions, great and small, creatively intertwined like words in a poem."[144] In that sense, such movements are "social poets" that, in their own way, work, propose, promote and liberate. They help make possible an integral human development that goes beyond "the idea of social policies being a policy *for* the poor, but never *with* the poor and never *of* the poor, much less part

---

[142] *Address to Participants in the World Meeting of Popular Movements* (28 October 2014): AAS 106 (2014), 858.

[143] Ibid.

[144] *Address to Participants in the World Meeting of Popular Movements* (5 November 2016): *L'Osservatore Romano*, 7-8 November 2016, pp. 4-5.

of a project that reunites peoples."[145] They may be troublesome, and certain "theorists" may find it hard to classify them, yet we must find the courage to acknowledge that, without them, "democracy atrophies, turns into a mere word, a formality; it loses its representative character and becomes disembodied, since it leaves out the people in their daily struggle for dignity, in the building of their future."[146]

INTERNATIONAL POWER

170. I would once more observe that "the financial crisis of 2007-08 provided an opportunity to develop a new economy, more attentive to ethical principles, and new ways of regulating speculative financial practices and virtual wealth. But the response to the crisis did not include rethinking the outdated criteria which continue to rule the world."[147] Indeed, it appears that the actual strategies developed worldwide in the wake of the crisis fostered greater individualism, less integration and increased freedom for the truly powerful, who always find a way to escape unscathed.

171. I would also insist that "to give to each his own – to cite the classic definition of justice – means that no human individual or group can consider itself absolute, entitled to bypass the dignity and the rights of other individuals or their social groupings. The effective distribution of power (especially political, economic, defence-related and technological power) among a plurality of subjects, and the creation of a juridical system for regulating claims and interests, are one concrete way of limiting power. Yet today's world presents us with many false rights

---

[145] Ibid.
[146] Ibid.
[147] Encyclical Letter *Laudato Si'* (24 May 2015), 189: AAS 107 (2015), 922.

and – at the same time – broad sectors which are vulnerable, victims of power badly exercised."[148]

172. The twenty-first century "is witnessing a weakening of the power of nation states, chiefly because the economic and financial sectors, being transnational, tend to prevail over the political. Given this situation, it is essential to devise stronger and more efficiently organized international institutions, with functionaries who are appointed fairly by agreement among national governments, and empowered to impose sanctions."[149] When we talk about the possibility of some form of world authority regulated by law,[150] we need not necessarily think of a personal authority. Still, such an authority ought at least to promote more effective world organizations, equipped with the power to provide for the global common good, the elimination of hunger and poverty and the sure defence of fundamental human rights.

173. In this regard, I would also note the need for a reform of "the United Nations Organization, and likewise of economic institutions and international finance, so that the concept of the family of nations can acquire real teeth."[151] Needless to say, this calls for clear legal limits to avoid power being co-opted only by a few countries and to prevent cultural impositions or a restriction of the basic freedoms of weaker nations on the basis of ideological differences. For "the international community is a juridical community founded on the sovereignty of each member state, without bonds of subordination that deny or limit its independence."[152] At the same time, "the work of the United

---

[148] *Address to the Members of the General Assembly of the United Nations Organization*, New York (25 September 2015): AAS 107 (2015), 1037.

[149] Encyclical Letter *Laudato Si'* (24 May 2015), 175: AAS 107 (2015), 916-917.

[150] Cf. BENEDICT XVI, Encyclical Letter *Caritas in Veritate* (29 June 2009), 67: AAS 101 (2009), 700-701.

[151] Ibid.: AAS 101 (2009), 700.

[152] PONTIFICAL COUNCIL FOR JUSTICE AND PEACE, *Compendium of the Social Doctrine of the Church*, 434.

Nations, according to the principles set forth in the Preamble and the first Articles of its founding Charter, can be seen as the development and promotion of the rule of law, based on the realization that justice is an essential condition for achieving the ideal of universal fraternity… There is a need to ensure the uncontested rule of law and tireless recourse to negotiation, mediation and arbitration, as proposed by the Charter of the United Nations, which constitutes truly a fundamental juridical norm."[153] There is need to prevent this Organization from being delegitimized, since its problems and shortcomings are capable of being jointly addressed and resolved.

174. Courage and generosity are needed in order freely to establish shared goals and to ensure the worldwide observance of certain essential norms. For this to be truly useful, it is essential to uphold "the need to be faithful to agreements undertaken (*pacta sunt servanda*),"[154] and to avoid the "temptation to appeal to the law of force rather than to the force of law."[155] This means reinforcing the "normative instruments for the peaceful resolution of controversies… so as to strengthen their scope and binding force."[156] Among these normative instruments, preference should be given to multilateral agreements between states, because, more than bilateral agreements, they guarantee the promotion of a truly universal common good and the protection of weaker states.

175. Providentially, many groups and organizations within civil society help to compensate for the shortcomings of the international community, its lack of coordination in complex

---

[153] *Address to the Members of the General Assembly of the United Nations Organization*, New York (25 September 2015): AAS 107 (2015), 1037, 1041.

[154] Pontifical Council for Justice and Peace, *Compendium of the Social Doctrine of the Church*, 437.

[155] SAINT JOHN PAUL II, *Message for the 2004 World Day of Peace*, 5: AAS 96 (2004), 117.

[156] Pontifical Council for Justice and Peace, *Compendium of the Social Doctrine of the Church*, 439.

situations, its lack of attention to fundamental human rights and to the critical needs of certain groups. Here we can see a concrete application of the principle of subsidiarity, which justifies the participation and activity of communities and organizations on lower levels as a means of integrating and complementing the activity of the state. These groups and organizations often carry out commendable efforts in the service of the common good and their members at times show true heroism, revealing something of the grandeur of which our humanity is still capable.

SOCIAL AND POLITICAL CHARITY

176. For many people today, politics is a distasteful word, often due to the mistakes, corruption and inefficiency of some politicians. There are also attempts to discredit politics, to replace it with economics or to twist it to one ideology or another. Yet can our world function without politics? Can there be an effective process of growth towards universal fraternity and social peace without a sound political life?[157]

The politics we need

177. Here I would once more observe that "politics must not be subject to the economy, nor should the economy be subject to the dictates of an efficiency-driven paradigm of technocracy."[158] Although misuse of power, corruption, disregard for law and inefficiency must clearly be rejected, "economics without politics cannot be justified, since this would make it impossible to favour other ways of handling the various aspects of the present crisis."[159] Instead, "what is needed is a politics which is far-sighted and capable of a new, integral and interdisciplinary

---

[157] Cf. SOCIAL COMMISSION OF THE BISHOPS OF FRANCE, Declaration *Réhabiliter la Politique* (17 February 1999).

[158] Encyclical Letter *Laudato Si'* (24 May 2015), 189: AAS 107 (2015), 922.

[159] Ibid., 196: AAS 107 (2015), 925.

approach to handling the different aspects of the crisis."[160] In other words, a "healthy politics... capable of reforming and coordinating institutions, promoting best practices and overcoming undue pressure and bureaucratic inertia."[161] We cannot expect economics to do this, nor can we allow economics to take over the real power of the state.

178. In the face of many petty forms of politics focused on immediate interests, I would repeat that "true statecraft is manifest when, in difficult times, we uphold high principles and think of the long-term common good. Political powers do not find it easy to assume this duty in the work of nation-building,"[162] much less in forging a common project for the human family, now and in the future. Thinking of those who will come after us does not serve electoral purposes, yet it is what authentic justice demands. As the Bishops of Portugal have taught, the earth "is lent to each generation, to be handed on to the generation that follows."[163]

179. Global society is suffering from grave structural deficiencies that cannot be resolved by piecemeal solutions or quick fixes. Much needs to change, through fundamental reform and major renewal. Only a healthy politics, involving the most diverse sectors and skills, is capable of overseeing this process. An economy that is an integral part of a political, social, cultural and popular programme directed to the common good could pave the way for "different possibilities which do not involve stifling human creativity and its ideals of progress, but rather directing that energy along new channels."[164]

---

[160] Ibid., 197: AAS 107 (2015), 925.

[161] Ibid., 181: AAS 107 (2015), 919.

[162] Ibid., 178: AAS 107 (2015), 918.

[163] PORTUGUESE BISHOPS' CONFERENCE, Pastoral Letter *Responsabilidade Solidária pelo Bem Comum* (15 September 2003), 20; cf. Encyclical Letter *Laudato Si'* (24 May 2015), 159: AAS 107 (2015), 911.

[164] Encyclical Letter *Laudato Si'* (24 May 2015), 191: AAS 107 (2015), 923.

Political love

180. Recognizing that all people are our brothers and sisters, and seeking forms of social friendship that include everyone, is not merely utopian. It demands a decisive commitment to devising effective means to this end. Any effort along these lines becomes a noble exercise of charity. For whereas individuals can help others in need, when they join together in initiating social processes of fraternity and justice for all, they enter the "field of charity at its most vast, namely political charity."[165] This entails working for a social and political order whose soul is social charity.[166] Once more, I appeal for a renewed appreciation of politics as "a lofty vocation and one of the highest forms of charity, inasmuch as it seeks the common good."[167]

181. Every commitment inspired by the Church's social doctrine is "derived from charity, which according to the teaching of Jesus is the synthesis of the entire Law (cf. *Mt* 22:36-40)."[168] This means acknowledging that "love, overflowing with small gestures of mutual care, is also civic and political, and it makes itself felt in every action that seeks to build a better world."[169] For this reason, charity finds expression not only in close and intimate relationships but also in "macro-relationships: social, economic and political."[170]

---

[165] PIUS XI, *Address to the Italian Catholic Federation of University Students* (18 December 1927): *L'Osservatore Romano,* 23 December 1927, p. 3.

[166] Cf. ID., Encyclical Letter *Quadragesimo Anno* (15 May 1931): AAS 23 (1931), 206-207.

[167] Apostolic Exhortation *Evangelii Gaudium* (24 November 2013), 205: AAS 105 (2013), 1106.

[168] Benedict XVI, Encyclical Letter *Caritas in Veritate* (29 June 2009), 2: AAS 101 (2009), 642.

[169] Encyclical Letter *Laudato Si'* (24 May 2015), 231: AAS 107 (2015), 937.

[170] Benedict XVI, Encyclical Letter *Caritas in Veritate* (29 June 2009), 2: AAS 101 (2009), 642.

182. This political charity is born of a social awareness that transcends every individualistic mindset: "'Social charity makes us love the common good,' it makes us effectively seek the good of all people, considered not only as individuals or private persons, but also in the social dimension that unites them."[171] Each of us is fully a person when we are part of a people; at the same time, there are no peoples without respect for the individuality of each person. "People" and "person" are correlative terms. Nonetheless, there are attempts nowadays to reduce persons to isolated individuals easily manipulated by powers pursuing spurious interests. Good politics will seek ways of building communities at every level of social life, in order to recalibrate and reorient globalization and thus avoid its disruptive effects.

Effective love

183. "Social love"[172] makes it possible to advance towards a civilization of love, to which all of us can feel called. Charity, with its impulse to universality, is capable of building a new world.[173] No mere sentiment, it is the best means of discovering effective paths of development for everyone. Social love is a "force capable of inspiring new ways of approaching the problems of today's world, of profoundly renewing structures, social organizations and legal systems from within."[174]

184. Charity is at the heart of every healthy and open society, yet today "it is easily dismissed as irrelevant for interpreting

---

[171] Pontifical Council for Justice and Peace, *Compendium of the Social Doctrine of the Church*, 207.

[172] SAINT JOHN PAUL II, Encyclical Letter *Redemptor Hominis* (4 March 1979), 15: AAS 71 (1979), 288.

[173] Cf. SAINT PAUL VI, Encyclical Letter *Populorum Progressio* (26 March 1967), 44: AAS 59 (1967), 279.

[174] Pontifical Council for Justice and Peace, *Compendium of the Social Doctrine of the Church*, 207.

and giving direction to moral responsibility."[175] Charity, when accompanied by a commitment to the truth, is much more than personal feeling, and consequently need not "fall prey to contingent subjective emotions and opinions."[176] Indeed its close relation to truth fosters its universality and preserves it from being "confined to a narrow field devoid of relationships."[177] Otherwise, it would be "excluded from the plans and processes of promoting human development of universal range, in dialogue between knowledge and praxis."[178] Without truth, emotion lacks relational and social content. Charity's openness to truth thus protects it from "a fideism that deprives it of its human and universal breadth."[179]

185. Charity needs the light of the truth that we constantly seek. "That light is both the light of reason and the light of faith,"[180] and does not admit any form of relativism. Yet it also respects the development of the sciences and their essential contribution to finding the surest and most practical means of achieving the desired results. For when the good of others is at stake, good intentions are not enough. Concrete efforts must be made to bring about whatever they and their nations need for the sake of their development.

THE EXERCISE OF POLITICAL LOVE

186. There is a kind of love that is "elicited": its acts proceed directly from the virtue of charity and are directed to individuals and peoples. There is also a "commanded" love, expressed in those acts of charity that spur people to create more sound

---

[175] Benedict XVI, Encyclical Letter *Caritas in Veritate* (29 June 2009), 2: AAS 101 (2009), 642.

[176] Ibid., 3: AAS 101 (2009), 643.

[177] Ibid., 4: AAS 101 (2009), 643.

[178] Ibid.

[179] Ibid., 3: AAS 101 (2009), 643.

[180] Ibid.: AAS 101 (2009), 642.

institutions, more just regulations, more supportive structures.[181] It follows that "it is an equally indispensable act of
love to strive to organize and structure society so that one's
neighbour will not find himself in poverty."[182] It is an act of
charity to assist someone suffering, but it is also an act of charity, even if we do not know that person, to work to change the
social conditions that caused his or her suffering. If someone
helps an elderly person cross a river, that is a fine act of charity. The politician, on the other hand, builds a bridge, and that
too is an act of charity. While one person can help another by
providing something to eat, the politician creates a job for that
other person, and thus practices a lofty form of charity that en-
nobles his or her political activity.

Sacrifices born of love

187. This charity, which is the spiritual heart of politics, is
always a preferential love shown to those in greatest need; it
undergirds everything we do on their behalf.[183] Only a gaze
transformed by charity can enable the dignity of others to be
recognized and, as a consequence, the poor to be acknowledged
and valued in their dignity, respected in their identity and culture, and thus truly integrated into society. That gaze is at the
heart of the authentic spirit of politics. It sees paths open up
that are different from those of a soulless pragmatism. It makes
us realize that "the scandal of poverty cannot be addressed

---

[181] Catholic moral doctrine, following the teaching of Saint Thomas Aquinas, distinguishes between "elicited" and "commanded" acts; cf. *Summa
Theologiae*, I-II, qq. 8-17; M. ZALBA, S.J., *Theologiae Moralis Summa.
Theologia Moralis Fundamentalis. Tractatus de Virtutibus Theologicis*, ed.
BAC, Madrid, 1952, vol. I, 69; A. ROYO MARÍN, *Teología de la Perfección
Cristiana*, ed. BAC, Madrid, 1962, 192-196.
[182] PONTIFICAL COUNCIL FOR JUSTICE AND PEACE, *Compendium
of the Social Doctrine of the Church*, 208.
[183] Cf. SAINT JOHN PAUL II, Encyclical Letter *Sollicitudo Rei Socialis* (30 December 1987), 42: AAS 80 (1988), 572-574; Encyclical Letter *Centesimus Annus* (1 May 1991), 11: AAS 83 (1991), 806-807.

by promoting strategies of containment that only tranquilize the poor and render them tame and inoffensive. How sad it is when we find, behind allegedly altruistic works, the other being reduced to passivity."[184] What are needed are new pathways of self-expression and participation in society. Education serves these by making it possible for each human being to shape his or her own future. Here too we see the importance of the principle of *subsidiarity*, which is inseparable from the principle of *solidarity*.

188. These considerations help us recognize the urgent need to combat all that threatens or violates fundamental human rights. Politicians are called to "tend to the needs of individuals and peoples. To tend those in need takes strength and tenderness, effort and generosity in the midst of a functionalistic and privatized mindset that inexorably leads to a 'throwaway culture'… It involves taking responsibility for the present with its situations of utter marginalization and anguish, and being capable of bestowing dignity upon it."[185] It will likewise inspire intense efforts to ensure that "everything be done to protect the status and dignity of the human person."[186] Politicians are doers, builders with ambitious goals, possessed of a broad, realistic and pragmatic gaze that looks beyond their own borders. Their biggest concern should not be about a drop in the polls, but about finding effective solutions to "the phenomenon of social and economic exclusion, with its baneful consequences: human trafficking, the marketing of human organs and tissues, the sexual exploitation of boys and girls, slave labour, including prostitution, the drug and weapons trade, terrorism and international organized crime. Such is the magnitude of these

---

[184] A*ddress to Participants in the World Meeting of Popular Movements* (28 October 2014): AAS 106 (2014), 852.

[185] *Address to the European Parliament*, Strasbourg (25 November 2014): AAS 106 (2014), 999.

[186] *Address at the Meeting with Authorities and the Diplomatic Corps in the Central African Republic*, Bangui (29 November 2015): AAS 107 (2015), 1320.

situations, and their toll in innocent lives, that we must avoid every temptation to fall into a declarationist nominalism that would assuage our consciences. We need to ensure that our institutions are truly effective in the struggle against all these scourges."[187] This includes taking intelligent advantage of the immense resources offered by technological development.

189. We are still far from a globalization of the most basic of human rights. That is why world politics needs to make the effective elimination of hunger one of its foremost and imperative goals. Indeed, "when financial speculation manipulates the price of food, treating it as just another commodity, millions of people suffer and die from hunger. At the same time, tons of food are thrown away. This constitutes a genuine scandal. Hunger is criminal; food is an inalienable right."[188] Often, as we carry on our semantic or ideological disputes, we allow our brothers and sisters to die of hunger and thirst, without shelter or access to health care. Alongside these basic needs that remain unmet, trafficking in persons represents another source of shame for humanity, one that international politics, moving beyond fine speeches and good intentions, must no longer tolerate. These things are essential; they can no longer be deferred.

A love that integrates and unites

190. Political charity is also expressed in a spirit of openness to everyone. Government leaders should be the first to make the sacrifices that foster encounter and to seek convergence on at least some issues. They should be ready to listen to other points of view and to make room for everyone. Through sacrifice and patience, they can help to create a beautiful polyhedral reality in which everyone has a place. Here, economic negotiations

---

[187] *Address to the United Nations Organization*, New York (25 September 2015): AAS 107 (2015), 1039.

[188] *Address to Participants in the World Meeting of Popular Movements* (28 October 2014): AAS 106 (2014), 853.

do not work. Something else is required: an exchange of gifts for the common good. It may seem naïve and utopian, yet we cannot renounce this lofty aim.

191. At a time when various forms of fundamentalist intolerance are damaging relationships between individuals, groups and peoples, let us be committed to living and teaching the value of respect for others, a love capable of welcoming differences, and the priority of the dignity of every human being over his or her ideas, opinions, practices and even sins. Even as forms of fanaticism, closedmindedness and social and cultural fragmentation proliferate in present-day society, a good politician will take the first step and insist that different voices be heard. Disagreements may well give rise to conflicts, but uniformity proves stifling and leads to cultural decay. May we not be content with being enclosed in one fragment of reality.

192. In this regard, Grand Imam Ahmad Al-Tayyeb and I have called upon "the architects of international policy and world economy to work strenuously to spread the culture of tolerance and of living together in peace; to intervene at the earliest opportunity to stop the shedding of innocent blood."[189] When a specific policy sows hatred and fear towards other nations in the name of its own country's welfare, there is need to be concerned, to react in time and immediately to correct the course.

FRUITFULNESS OVER RESULTS

193. Apart from their tireless activity, politicians are also men and women. They are called to practice love in their daily interpersonal relationships. As persons, they need to consider that "the modern world, with its technical advances, tends in-

---

[189] *Document on Human Fraternity for World Peace and Living Together*, Abu Dhabi (4 February 2019): *L'Osservatore Romano*, 4-5 February 2019, p. 6.

creasingly to functionalize the satisfaction of human desires, now classified and subdivided among different services. Less and less will people be called by name, less and less will this unique being be treated as a person with his or her own feelings, sufferings, problems, joys and family. Their illnesses will be known only in order to cure them, their financial needs only to provide for them, their lack of a home only to give them lodging, their desires for recreation and entertainment only to satisfy them." Yet it must never be forgotten that "loving the most insignificant of human beings as a brother, as if there were no one else in the world but him, cannot be considered a waste of time."[190]

194. Politics too must make room for a tender love of others. "What is tenderness? It is love that draws near and becomes real. A movement that starts from our heart and reaches the eyes, the ears and the hands… Tenderness is the path of choice for the strongest, most courageous men and women."[191] Amid the daily concerns of political life, "the smallest, the weakest, the poorest should touch our hearts: indeed, they have a 'right' to appeal to our heart and soul. They are our brothers and sisters, and as such we must love and care for them."[192]

195. All this can help us realize that what is important is not constantly achieving great results, since these are not always possible. In political activity, we should remember that, "appearances notwithstanding, every person is immensely holy and deserves our love. Consequently, if I can help at least one person to have a better life, that already justifies the offering of my life. It is a wonderful thing to be God's faithful people. We achieve fulfilment when we break down walls and our

[190] RENÉ VOILLAUME, *Frères de tous*, ed. Cerf, Paris, 1968, 12-13.

[191] *Video Message to the TED Conference in Vancouver* (26 April 2017): *L'Osservatore Romano*, 27 April 2017, p. 7.

[192] *General Audience* (18 February 2015): *L'Osservatore Romano*, 19 February 2015, p. 8.

hearts are filled with faces and names!"[193] The great goals of our dreams and plans may only be achieved in part. Yet beyond this, those who love, and who no longer view politics merely as a quest for power, "may be sure that none of our acts of love will be lost, nor any of our acts of sincere concern for others. No single act of love for God will be lost, no generous effort is meaningless, no painful endurance is wasted. All of these encircle our world like a vital force."[194]

196. For this reason, it is truly noble to place our hope in the hidden power of the seeds of goodness we sow, and thus to initiate processes whose fruits will be reaped by others. Good politics combines love with hope and with confidence in the reserves of goodness present in human hearts. Indeed, "authentic political life, built upon respect for law and frank dialogue between individuals, is constantly renewed whenever there is a realization that every woman and man, and every new generation, brings the promise of new relational, intellectual, cultural and spiritual energies."[195]

197. Viewed in this way, politics is something more noble than posturing, marketing and media spin. These sow nothing but division, conflict and a bleak cynicism incapable of mobilizing people to pursue a common goal. At times, in thinking of the future, we do well to ask ourselves, "Why I am doing this?," "What is my real aim?" For as time goes on, reflecting on the past, the questions will not be: "How many people endorsed me?," "How many voted for me?," "How many had a positive image of me?" The real, and potentially painful, questions will be, "How much love did I put into my work?" "What did I do for the progress of our people?" "What mark did I leave on

---

[193] Apostolic Exhortation *Evangelii Gaudium* (24 November 2013), 274: AAS 105 (2013), 1130.

[194] Ibid., 279: AAS 105 (2013), 1132.

[195] *Message for the 2019 World Day of Peace* (8 December 2018), 5: *L'Osservatore Romano*, 19 December 2018, p. 8.

the life of society?" "What real bonds did I create?" "What positive forces did I unleash?" "How much social peace did I sow?" "What good did I achieve in the position that was entrusted to me?"

CHAPTER SIX

DIALOGUE AND FRIENDSHIP IN SOCIETY

198. Approaching, speaking, listening, looking at, coming to know and understand one another, and to find common ground: all these things are summed up in the one word "dialogue." If we want to encounter and help one another, we have to dialogue. There is no need for me to stress the benefits of dialogue. I have only to think of what our world would be like without the patient dialogue of the many generous persons who keep families and communities together. Unlike disagreement and conflict, persistent and courageous dialogue does not make headlines, but quietly helps the world to live much better than we imagine.

SOCIAL DIALOGUE FOR A NEW CULTURE

199. Some people attempt to flee from reality, taking refuge in their own little world; others react to it with destructive violence. Yet "between selfish indifference and violent protest there is always another possible option: that of dialogue. Dialogue between generations; dialogue among our people, for we are that people; readiness to give and receive, while remaining open to the truth. A country flourishes when constructive dialogue occurs between its many rich cultural components: popular culture, university culture, youth culture, artistic culture, technological culture, economic culture, family culture and media culture."[196]

---

[196] *Meeting with Brazilian Political, Economic and Cultural Leaders*, Rio de Janeiro, Brazil (27 July 2013): AAS 105 (2013), 683-684.

200. Dialogue is often confused with something quite different: the feverish exchange of opinions on social networks, frequently based on media information that is not always reliable. These exchanges are merely parallel monologues. They may attract some attention by their sharp and aggressive tone. But monologues engage no one, and their content is frequently self-serving and contradictory.

201. Indeed, the media's noisy potpourri of facts and opinions is often an obstacle to dialogue, since it lets everyone cling stubbornly to his or her own ideas, interests and choices, with the excuse that everyone else is wrong. It becomes easier to discredit and insult opponents from the outset than to open a respectful dialogue aimed at achieving agreement on a deeper level. Worse, this kind of language, usually drawn from media coverage of political campaigns, has become so widespread as to be part of daily conversation. Discussion is often manipulated by powerful special interests that seek to tilt public opinion unfairly in their favour. This kind of manipulation can be exercised not only by governments, but also in economics, politics, communications, religion and in other spheres. Attempts can be made to justify or excuse it when it tends to serve one's own economic or ideological interests, but sooner or later it turns against those very interests.

202. Lack of dialogue means that in these individual sectors people are concerned not for the common good, but for the benefits of power or, at best, for ways to impose their own ideas. Round tables thus become mere negotiating sessions, in which individuals attempt to seize every possible advantage, rather than cooperating in the pursuit of the common good. The heroes of the future will be those who can break with this unhealthy mindset and determine respectfully to promote truthfulness, aside from personal interest. God willing, such heroes are quietly emerging, even now, in the midst of our society.

Building together

203. Authentic social dialogue involves the ability to respect the other's point of view and to admit that it may include legitimate convictions and concerns. Based on their identity and experience, others have a contribution to make, and it is desirable that they should articulate their positions for the sake of a more fruitful public debate. When individuals or groups are consistent in their thinking, defend their values and convictions, and develop their arguments, this surely benefits society. Yet, this can only occur to the extent that there is genuine dialogue and openness to others. Indeed, "in a true spirit of dialogue, we grow in our ability to grasp the significance of what others say and do, even if we cannot accept it as our own conviction. In this way, it becomes possible to be frank and open about our beliefs, while continuing to discuss, to seek points of contact, and above all, to work and struggle together."[197] Public discussion, if it truly makes room for everyone and does not manipulate or conceal information, is a constant stimulus to a better grasp of the truth, or at least its more effective expression. It keeps different sectors from becoming complacent and self-centred in their outlook and their limited concerns. Let us not forget that "differences are creative; they create tension and in the resolution of tension lies humanity's progress."[198]

204. There is a growing conviction that, together with specialized scientific advances, we are in need of greater interdisciplinary communication. Although reality is one, it can be approached from various angles and with different methodologies. There is a risk that a single scientific advance will be seen as the only possible lens for viewing a particular aspect of life, society and the world. Researchers who are expert in

---

[197] Apostolic Exhortation *Querida Amazonia* (2 February 2020), 108.
[198] From the film *Pope Francis: A Man of His Word*, by Wim Wenders (2018).

their own field, yet also familiar with the findings of other sciences and disciplines, are in a position to discern other aspects of the object of their study and thus to become open to a more comprehensive and integral knowledge of reality.

205. In today's globalized world, "the media can help us to feel closer to one another, creating a sense of the unity of the human family which in turn can inspire solidarity and serious efforts to ensure a more dignified life for all... The media can help us greatly in this, especially nowadays, when the networks of human communication have made unprecedented advances. The internet, in particular, offers immense possibilities for encounter and solidarity. This is something truly good, a gift from God."[199] We need constantly to ensure that present-day forms of communication are in fact guiding us to generous encounter with others, to honest pursuit of the whole truth, to service, to closeness to the underprivileged and to the promotion of the common good. As the Bishops of Australia have pointed out, we cannot accept "a digital world designed to exploit our weaknesses and bring out the worst in people."[200]

The BASIS of Consensus

206. The solution is not relativism. Under the guise of tolerance, relativism ultimately leaves the interpretation of moral values to those in power, to be defined as they see fit. "In the absence of objective truths or sound principles other than the satisfaction of our own desires and immediate needs... we should not think that political efforts or the force of law will be sufficient... When the culture itself is corrupt, and objective truth and universally valid principles are no longer upheld, then

---

[199] *Message for the 2014 World Communications Day* (24 January 2014): AAS 106 (2014), 113.

[200] AUSTRALIAN CATHOLIC BISHOPS' CONFERENCE, Commission for Social Justice, Mission and Service, *Making It Real: Genuine Human Encounter in Our Digital World* (November 2019).

laws can only be seen as arbitrary impositions or obstacles to be avoided."[201]

207. Is it possible to be concerned for truth, to seek the truth that responds to life's deepest meaning? What is law without the conviction, born of age-old reflection and great wisdom, that each human being is sacred and inviolable? If society is to have a future, it must respect the truth of our human dignity and submit to that truth. Murder is not wrong simply because it is socially unacceptable and punished by law, but because of a deeper conviction. This is a non-negotiable truth attained by the use of reason and accepted in conscience. A society is noble and decent not least for its support of the pursuit of truth and its adherence to the most basic of truths.

208. We need to learn how to unmask the various ways that the truth is manipulated, distorted and concealed in public and private discourse. What we call "truth" is not only the reporting of facts and events, such as we find in the daily papers. It is primarily the search for the solid foundations sustaining our decisions and our laws. This calls for acknowledging that the human mind is capable of transcending immediate concerns and grasping certain truths that are unchanging, as true now as in the past. As it peers into human nature, reason discovers universal values derived from that same nature.

209. Otherwise, is it not conceivable that those fundamental human rights which we now consider unassailable will be denied by those in power, once they have gained the "consensus" of an apathetic or intimidated population? Nor would a mere consensus between different nations, itself equally open to manipulation, suffice to protect them. We have ample evidence of the great good of which we are capable, yet we also have to acknowledge our inherent destructiveness. Is not the

---

[201] Encyclical Letter *Laudato Si'* (24 May 2015), 123: AAS 107 (2015), 896.

indifference and the heartless individualism into which we have fallen also a result of our sloth in pursuing higher values, values that transcend our immediate needs? Relativism always brings the risk that some or other alleged truth will be imposed by the powerful or the clever. Yet, "when it is a matter of the moral norms prohibiting intrinsic evil, there are no privileges or exceptions for anyone. It makes no difference whether one is the master of the world or the 'poorest of the poor' on the face of the earth. Before the demands of morality we are all absolutely equal."[202]

210. What is now happening, and drawing us into a perverse and barren way of thinking, is the reduction of ethics and politics to physics. Good and evil no longer exist in themselves; there is only a calculus of benefits and burdens. As a result of the displacement of moral reasoning, the law is no longer seen as reflecting a fundamental notion of justice but as mirroring notions currently in vogue. Breakdown ensues: everything is "leveled down" by a superficial bartered consensus. In the end, the law of the strongest prevails.

Consensus and truth

211. In a pluralistic society, dialogue is the best way to realize what ought always to be affirmed and respected apart from any ephemeral consensus. Such dialogue needs to be enriched and illumined by clear thinking, rational arguments, a variety of perspectives and the contribution of different fields of knowledge and points of view. Nor can it exclude the conviction that it is possible to arrive at certain fundamental truths always to be upheld. Acknowledging the existence of certain enduring values, however demanding it may be to discern them, makes for a robust and solid social ethics. Once those fundamental values are acknowledged and adopted through dialogue and

---

[202] SAINT JOHN PAUL II, Encyclical Letter *Veritatis Splendor* (6 August 1993), 96: AAS 85 (1993), 1209.

consensus, we realize that they rise above consensus; they transcend our concrete situations and remain non-negotiable. Our understanding of their meaning and scope can increase – and in that respect, consensus is a dynamic reality – but in themselves, they are held to be enduring by virtue of their inherent meaning.

212. If something always serves the good functioning of society, is it not because, lying beyond it, there is an enduring truth accessible to the intellect? Inherent in the nature of human beings and society there exist certain basic structures to support our development and survival. Certain requirements thus ensue, and these can be discovered through dialogue, even though, strictly speaking, they are not created by consensus. The fact that certain rules are indispensable for the very life of society is a sign that they are good in and of themselves. There is no need, then, to oppose the interests of society, consensus and the reality of objective truth. These three realities can be harmonized whenever, through dialogue, people are unafraid to get to the heart of an issue.

213. The dignity of others is to be respected in all circumstances, not because that dignity is something we have invented or imagined, but because human beings possess an intrinsic worth superior to that of material objects and contingent situations. This requires that they be treated differently. That every human being possesses an inalienable dignity is a truth that corresponds to human nature apart from all cultural change. For this reason, human beings have the same inviolable dignity in every age of history and no one can consider himself or herself authorized by particular situations to deny this conviction or to act against it. The intellect can investigate the reality of things through reflection, experience and dialogue, and come to recognize in that reality, which transcends it, the basis of certain universal moral demands.

214. To agnostics, this foundation could prove sufficient to confer a solid and stable universal validity on basic and non-

negotiable ethical principles that could serve to prevent further catastrophes. As believers, we are convinced that human nature, as the source of ethical principles, was created by God, and that ultimately it is he who gives those principles their solid foundation.[203] This does not result in an ethical rigidity nor does it lead to the imposition of any one moral system, since fundamental and universally valid moral principles can be embodied in different practical rules. Thus, room for dialogue will always exist.

A NEW CULTURE

215. "Life, for all its confrontations, is the art of encounter."[204] I have frequently called for the growth of a culture of encounter capable of transcending our differences and divisions. This means working to create a many-faceted polyhedron whose different sides form a variegated unity, in which "the whole is greater than the part."[205] The image of a polyhedron can represent a society where differences coexist, complementing, enriching and reciprocally illuminating one another, even amid disagreements and reservations. Each of us can learn something from others. No one is useless and no one is expendable. This also means finding ways to include those on the peripheries of life. For they have another way of looking at things; they see aspects of reality that are invisible to the centres of power where weighty decisions are made.

Encounter that becomes culture

216. The word "culture" points to something deeply embedded within a people, its most cherished convictions and its way of

---

[203] SAINT JOHN PAUL II, Encyclical Letter *Veritatis Splendor* (6 August 1993), 96: AAS 85 (1993), 1209.

[204] VINICIUS DE MORAES, *Samba da Benção,* from the recording *Um encontro no Au bon Gourmet*, Rio de Janeiro (2 August 1962).

[205] Apostolic Exhortation *Evangelii Gaudium* (24 November 2013), 237: AAS 105 (2013), 1116.

life. A people's "culture" is more than an abstract idea. It has to do with their desires, their interests and ultimately the way they live their lives. To speak of a "culture of encounter" means that we, as a people, should be passionate about meeting others, seeking points of contact, building bridges, planning a project that includes everyone. This becomes an aspiration and a style of life. The subject of this culture is the people, not simply one part of society that would pacify the rest with the help of professional and media resources.

217. Social peace demands hard work, craftsmanship. It would be easier to keep freedoms and differences in check with cleverness and a few resources. But such a peace would be superficial and fragile, not the fruit of a culture of encounter that brings enduring stability. Integrating differences is a much more difficult and slow process, yet it is the guarantee of a genuine and lasting peace. That peace is not achieved by recourse only to those who are pure and untainted, since "even people who can be considered questionable on account of their errors have something to offer which must not be overlooked."[206] Nor does it come from ignoring social demands or quelling disturbances, since it is not "a consensus on paper or a transient peace for a contented minority."[207] What is important is to create *processes* of encounter, processes that build a people that can accept differences. Let us arm our children with the weapons of dialogue! Let us teach them to fight the good fight of the culture of encounter!

The joy of acknowledging others

218. All this calls for the ability to recognize other people's right to be themselves and to be different. This recognition, as it becomes a culture, makes possible the creation of a social covenant. Without it, subtle ways can be found to make others

---

[206] Ibid., 236: AAS 105 (2013), 1115.
[207] Ibid., 218: AAS 105 (2013), 1110.

insignificant, irrelevant, of no value to society. While rejecting certain visible forms of violence, another more insidious kind of violence can take root: the violence of those who despise people who are different, especially when their demands in any way compromise their own particular interests.

219. When one part of society exploits all that the world has to offer, acting as if the poor did not exist, there will eventually be consequences. Sooner or later, ignoring the existence and rights of others will erupt in some form of violence, often when least expected. Liberty, equality and fraternity can remain lofty ideals unless they apply to everyone. Encounter cannot take place only between the holders of economic, political or academic power. Genuine social encounter calls for a dialogue that engages the culture shared by the majority of the population. It often happens that good ideas are not accepted by the poorer sectors of society because they are presented in a cultural garb that is not their own and with which they cannot identify. A realistic and inclusive social covenant must also be a "cultural covenant," one that respects and acknowledges the different worldviews, cultures and lifestyles that coexist in society.

220. Indigenous peoples, for example, are not opposed to progress, yet theirs is a different notion of progress, often more humanistic than the modern culture of developed peoples. Theirs is not a culture meant to benefit the powerful, those driven to create for themselves a kind of earthly paradise. Intolerance and lack of respect for indigenous popular cultures is a form of violence grounded in a cold and judgmental way of viewing them. No authentic, profound and enduring change is possible unless it starts from the different cultures, particularly those of the poor. A cultural covenant eschews a monolithic understanding of the identity of a particular place; it entails respect for diversity by offering opportunities for advancement and social integration to all.

221. Such a covenant also demands the realization that some things may have to be renounced for the common good. No one

can possess the whole truth or satisfy his or her every desire, since that pretension would lead to nullifying others by denying their rights. A false notion of tolerance has to give way to a dialogic realism on the part of men and women who remain faithful to their own principles while recognizing that others also have the right to do likewise. This is the genuine acknowledgment of the other that is made possible by love alone. We have to stand in the place of others, if we are to discover what is genuine, or at least understandable, in their motivations and concerns.

RECOVERING KINDNESS

222. Consumerist individualism has led to great injustice. Other persons come to be viewed simply as obstacles to our own serene existence; we end up treating them as annoyances and we become increasingly aggressive. This is even more the case in times of crisis, catastrophe and hardship, when we are tempted to think in terms of the old saying, "every man for himself." Yet even then, we can choose to cultivate kindness. Those who do so become stars shining in the midst of darkness.

223. Saint Paul describes kindness as a fruit of the Holy Spirit (*Gal* 5:22). He uses the Greek word *chrestótes*, which describes an attitude that is gentle, pleasant and supportive, not rude or coarse. Individuals who possess this quality help make other people's lives more bearable, especially by sharing the weight of their problems, needs and fears. This way of treating others can take different forms: an act of kindness, a concern not to offend by word or deed, a readiness to alleviate their burdens. It involves "speaking words of comfort, strength, consolation and encouragement" and not "words that demean, sadden, anger or show scorn."[208]

---

[208] Apostolic Exhortation *Amoris Laetitia* (19 March 2016), 100: AAS 108 (2016), 351.

224. Kindness frees us from the cruelty that at times infects human relationships, from the anxiety that prevents us from thinking of others, from the frantic flurry of activity that forgets that others also have a right to be happy. Often nowadays we find neither the time nor the energy to stop and be kind to others, to say "excuse me," "pardon me," "thank you." Yet every now and then, miraculously, a kind person appears and is willing to set everything else aside in order to show interest, to give the gift of a smile, to speak a word of encouragement, to listen amid general indifference. If we make a daily effort to do exactly this, we can create a healthy social atmosphere in which misunderstandings can be overcome and conflict forestalled. Kindness ought to be cultivated; it is no superficial bourgeois virtue. Precisely because it entails esteem and respect for others, once kindness becomes a culture within society it transforms lifestyles, relationships and the ways ideas are discussed and compared. Kindness facilitates the quest for consensus; it opens new paths where hostility and conflict would burn all bridges.

CHAPTER SEVEN

PATHS OF RENEWED ENCOUNTER

225. In many parts of the world, there is a need for paths of peace to heal open wounds. There is also a need for peacemakers, men and women prepared to work boldly and creatively to initiate processes of healing and renewed encounter.

STARTING ANEW FROM THE TRUTH

226. Renewed encounter does not mean returning to a time prior to conflicts. All of us change over time. Pain and conflict transform us. We no longer have use for empty diplomacy, dissimulation, double-speak, hidden agendas and good man-

ners that mask reality. Those who were fierce enemies have to speak from the stark and clear truth. They have to learn how to cultivate a penitential memory, one that can accept the past in order not to cloud the future with their own regrets, problems and plans. Only by basing themselves on the historical truth of events will they be able to make a broad and persevering effort to understand one another and to strive for a new synthesis for the good of all. Every "peace process requires enduring commitment. It is a patient effort to seek truth and justice, to honour the memory of victims and to open the way, step by step, to a shared hope stronger than the desire for vengeance."[209] As the Bishops of the Congo have said with regard to one recurring conflict: "Peace agreements on paper will not be enough. We will have to go further, by respecting the demands of truth regarding the origins of this recurring crisis. The people have the right to know what happened."[210]

227. "Truth, in fact, is an inseparable companion of justice and mercy. All three together are essential to building peace; each, moreover, prevents the other from being altered... Truth should not lead to revenge, but rather to reconciliation and forgiveness. Truth means telling families torn apart by pain what happened to their missing relatives. Truth means confessing what happened to minors recruited by cruel and violent people. Truth means recognizing the pain of women who are victims of violence and abuse... Every act of violence committed against a human being is a wound in humanity's flesh; every violent death diminishes us as people... Violence leads to more violence, hatred to more hatred, death to more death. We must break this cycle which seems inescapable."[211]

---

[209] *Message for the 2020 World Day of Peace* (8 December 2019), 2: *L'Osservatore Romano*, 13 December 2019, p. 8.

[210] EPISCOPAL CONFERENCE OF THE CONGO, *Message au Peuple de Dieu et aux femmes et aux hommes de bonne volonté* (9 May 2018).

[211] *Address at the National Reconciliation Encunter*, Villavicencio, Colombia (8 September 2017): AAS 109 (2017), 1063-1064, 1066.

THE ART AND ARCHITECTURE OF PEACE

228. The path to peace does not mean making society blandly uniform, but getting people to work together, side-by-side, in pursuing goals that benefit everyone. A wide variety of practical proposals and diverse experiences can help achieve shared objectives and serve the common good. The problems that a society is experiencing need to be clearly identified, so that the existence of different ways of understanding and resolving them can be appreciated. The path to social unity always entails acknowledging the possibility that others have, at least in part, a legitimate point of view, something worthwhile to contribute, even if they were in error or acted badly. "We should never confine others to what they may have said or done, but value them for the promise that they embody,"[212] a promise that always brings with it a spark of new hope.

229. The Bishops of South Africa have pointed out that true reconciliation is achieved proactively, "by forming a new society, a society based on service to others, rather than the desire to dominate; a society based on sharing what one has with others, rather than the selfish scramble by each for as much wealth as possible; a society in which the value of being together as human beings is ultimately more important than any lesser group, whether it be family, nation, race or culture."[213] As the Bishops of South Korea have pointed out, true peace "can be achieved only when we strive for justice through dialogue, pursuing reconciliation and mutual development."[214]

---

[212] *Message for the 2020 World Day of Peace* (8 December 2019), 3: *L'Osservatore Romano*, 13 December 2019, p. 8.

[213] SOUTHERN AFRICAN CATHOLIC BISHOPS' CONFERENCE, *Pastoral Letter on Christian Hope in the Current Crisis* (May 1986).

[214] CATHOLIC BISHOPS' CONFERENCE OF KOREA, *Appeal of the Catholic Church in Korea for Peace on the Korean Peninsula* (15 August 2017).

230. Working to overcome our divisions without losing our identity as individuals presumes that a basic sense of belonging is present in everyone. Indeed, "society benefits when each person and social group feels truly at home. In a family, parents, grandparents and children all feel at home; no one is excluded. If someone has a problem, even a serious one, even if he brought it upon himself, the rest of the family comes to his assistance; they support him. His problems are theirs… In families, everyone contributes to the common purpose; everyone works for the common good, not denying each person's individuality but encouraging and supporting it. They may quarrel, but there is something that does not change: the family bond. Family disputes are always resolved afterwards. The joys and sorrows of each of its members are felt by all. That is what it means to be a family! If only we could view our political opponents or neighbours in the same way that we view our children or our spouse, mother or father! How good would this be! Do we love our society or is it still something remote, something anonymous that does not involve us, something to which we are not committed?"[215]

231. Negotiation often becomes necessary for shaping concrete paths to peace. Yet the processes of change that lead to lasting peace are crafted above all by peoples; each individual can act as an effective leaven by the way he or she lives each day. Great changes are not produced behind desks or in offices. This means that "everyone has a fundamental role to play in a single great creative project: to write a new page of history, a page full of hope, peace and reconciliation."[216] There is an "architecture" of peace, to which different institutions of society contribute, each according to its own area of expertise, but there is also

---

[215] *Meeting with Political, Economic and Civic Leaders*, Quito, Ecuador (7 July 2015): *L'Osservatore Romano*, 9 July 2015, p. 9.

[216] *Interreligious Meeting with Youth*, Maputo, Mozambique (5 September 2019): *L'Osservatore Romano*, 6 September 2019, p. 7.

an "art" of peace that involves us all. From the various peace processes that have taken place in different parts of the world, "we have learned that these ways of making peace, of placing reason above revenge, of the delicate harmony between politics and law, cannot ignore the involvement of ordinary people. Peace is not achieved by normative frameworks and institutional arrangements between well-meaning political or economic groups... It is always helpful to incorporate into our peace processes the experience of those sectors that have often been overlooked, so that communities themselves can influence the development of a collective memory."[217]

232. There is no end to the building of a country's social peace; rather, it is "an open-ended endeavour, a never-ending task that demands the commitment of everyone and challenges us to work tirelessly to build the unity of the nation. Despite obstacles, differences and varying perspectives on the way to achieve peaceful coexistence, this task summons us to persevere in the struggle to promote a 'culture of encounter.' This requires us to place at the centre of all political, social and economic activity the human person, who enjoys the highest dignity, and respect for the common good. May this determination help us flee from the temptation for revenge and the satisfaction of short-term partisan interests."[218] Violent public demonstrations, on one side or the other, do not help in finding solutions. Mainly because, as the Bishops of Colombia have rightly noted, the "origins and objectives of civil demonstrations are not always clear; certain forms of political manipulation are present and in some cases they have been exploited for partisan interests."[219]

---

[217] *Homily*, Cartagena de Indias, Colombia (10 September 2017): AAS 109 (2017), 1086.

[218] *Meeting with Authorities, the Diplomatic Corps and Representatives of Civil Society*, Bogotá, Colombia (7 September 2017): AAS 109 (2017), 1029.

[219] BISHOPS' CONFERENCE OF COLOMBIA, *Por el bien de Colombia: diálogo, reconciliación y desarrollo integral* (26 November 2019), 4.

Beginning with the least

233. Building social friendship does not only call for rapprochement between groups who took different sides at some troubled period of history, but also for a renewed encounter with the most impoverished and vulnerable sectors of society. For peace "is not merely absence of war but a tireless commitment – especially on the part of those of us charged with greater responsibility – to recognize, protect and concretely restore the dignity, so often overlooked or ignored, of our brothers and sisters, so that they can see themselves as the principal protagonists of the destiny of their nation."[220]

234. Often, the more vulnerable members of society are the victims of unfair generalizations. If at times the poor and the dispossessed react with attitudes that appear antisocial, we should realize that in many cases those reactions are born of a history of scorn and social exclusion. The Latin American Bishops have observed that "only the closeness that makes us friends can enable us to appreciate deeply the values of the poor today, their legitimate desires, and their own manner of living the faith. The option for the poor should lead us to friendship with the poor."[221]

235. Those who work for tranquil social coexistence should never forget that inequality and lack of integral human development make peace impossible. Indeed, "without equal opportunities, different forms of aggression and conflict will find a fertile terrain for growth and eventually explode. When a society – whether local, national or global – is willing to leave a part of itself on the fringes, no political programmes

---

[220] *Meeting with the Authorities, Civil Society and the Diplomatic Corps*, Maputo, Mozambique (5 September 2019): *L'Osservatore Romano*, 6 September 2019, p. 6.

[221] FIFTH GENERAL CONFERENCE OF THE LATIN AMERICAN AND CARIBBEAN BISHOPS, *Aparecida Document* (29 June 2007), 398.

or resources spent on law enforcement or surveillance systems can indefinitely guarantee tranquility."[222] If we have to begin anew, it must always be from the least of our brothers and sisters.

THE VALUE AND MEANING OF FORGIVENESS

236. There are those who prefer not to talk of reconciliation, for they think that conflict, violence and breakdown are part of the normal functioning of a society. In any human group there are always going to be more or less subtle power struggles between different parties. Others think that promoting forgiveness means yielding ground and influence to others. For this reason, they feel it is better to keep things as they are, maintaining a balance of power between differing groups. Still others believe that reconciliation is a sign of weakness; incapable of truly serious dialogue, they choose to avoid problems by ignoring injustices. Unable to deal with problems, they opt for an apparent peace.

Inevitable conflict

237. Forgiveness and reconciliation are central themes in Christianity and, in various ways, in other religions. Yet there is a risk that an inadequate understanding and presentation of these profound convictions can lead to fatalism, apathy and injustice, or even intolerance and violence.

238. Jesus never promoted violence or intolerance. He openly condemned the use of force to gain power over others: "You know that the rulers of the Gentiles lord it over them, and their great ones are tyrants over them. It will not be so among

---

[222] Apostolic Exhortation *Evangelii Gaudium* (24 November 2013), 59: AAS 105 (2013), 1044.

you" (*Mt* 20:25-26). Instead, the Gospel tells us to forgive "seventy times seven" (*Mt* 18:22) and offers the example of the unmerciful servant who was himself forgiven, yet unable to forgive others in turn (cf. *Mt* 18:23-35).

239. Reading other texts of the New Testament, we can see how the early Christian communities, living in a pagan world marked by widespread corruption and aberrations, sought to show unfailing patience, tolerance and understanding. Some texts are very clear in this regard: we are told to admonish our opponents "with gentleness" (*2 Tim* 2:25) and encouraged "to speak evil of no one, to avoid quarreling, to be gentle, and to show every courtesy to everyone. For we ourselves were once foolish" (*Tit* 3:2-3). The Acts of the Apostles notes that the disciples, albeit persecuted by some of the authorities, "had favour with all the people" (2:47; cf. 4:21.33; 5:13).

240. Yet when we reflect upon forgiveness, peace and social harmony, we also encounter the jarring saying of Christ: "Do not think that I have come to bring peace to the earth; I have not come to bring peace, but a sword. For I have come to set a man against his father, and a daughter against her mother, and a daughter-in-law against her mother-in-law; and a man's foes will be members of his own household" (*Mt* 10:34-36). These words need to be understood in the context of the chapter in which they are found, where it is clear that Jesus is speaking of fidelity to our decision to follow him; we are not to be ashamed of that decision, even if it entails hardships of various sorts, and even our loved ones refuse to accept it. Christ's words do not encourage us to seek conflict, but simply to endure it when it inevitably comes, lest deference to others, for the sake of supposed peace in our families or society, should detract from our own fidelity. Saint John Paul II observed that the Church "does not intend to condemn every possible form of social conflict. The Church is well aware that in the course of history conflicts of interest between different social groups inevitably arise, and

that in the face of such conflicts Christians must often take a position, honestly and decisively."[223]

Legitimate conflict and forgiveness

241. Nor does this mean calling for forgiveness when it involves renouncing our own rights, confronting corrupt officials, criminals or those who would debase our dignity. We are called to love everyone, without exception; at the same time, loving an oppressor does not mean allowing him to keep oppressing us, or letting him think that what he does is acceptable. On the contrary, true love for an oppressor means seeking ways to make him cease his oppression; it means stripping him of a power that he does not know how to use, and that diminishes his own humanity and that of others. Forgiveness does not entail allowing oppressors to keep trampling on their own dignity and that of others, or letting criminals continue their wrongdoing. Those who suffer injustice have to defend strenuously their own rights and those of their family, precisely because they must preserve the dignity they have received as a loving gift from God. If a criminal has harmed me or a loved one, no one can forbid me from demanding justice and ensuring that this person – or anyone else – will not harm me, or others, again. This is entirely just; forgiveness does not forbid it but actually demands it.

242. The important thing is not to fuel anger, which is unhealthy for our own soul and the soul of our people, or to become obsessed with taking revenge and destroying the other. No one achieves inner peace or returns to a normal life in that way. The truth is that "no family, no group of neighbours, no ethnic group, much less a nation, has a future if the force that unites them, brings them together and resolves their differences

---

[223] Encyclical Letter *Centesimus Annus* (1 May 1991), 14: AAS 83 (1991), 810.

is vengeance and hatred. We cannot come to terms and unite for the sake of revenge, or treating others with the same violence with which they treated us, or plotting opportunities for retaliation under apparently legal auspices."[224] Nothing is gained this way and, in the end, everything is lost.

243. To be sure, "it is no easy task to overcome the bitter legacy of injustices, hostility and mistrust left by conflict. It can only be done by overcoming evil with good (cf. *Rom* 12:21) and by cultivating those virtues which foster reconciliation, solidarity and peace."[225] In this way, "persons who nourish goodness in their heart find that such goodness leads to a peaceful conscience and to profound joy, even in the midst of difficulties and misunderstandings. Even when affronted, goodness is never weak but rather, shows its strength by refusing to take revenge."[226] Each of us should realize that "even the harsh judgment I hold in my heart against my brother or my sister, the open wound that was never cured, the offense that was never forgiven, the rancour that is only going to hurt me, are all instances of a struggle that I carry within me, a little flame deep in my heart that needs to be extinguished before it turns into a great blaze."[227]

The best way to move on

244. When conflicts are not resolved but kept hidden or buried in the past, silence can lead to complicity in grave misdeeds

---

[224] *Homily at Mass for the Progress of Peoples*, Maputo, Mozambique (6 September 2019): *L'Osservatore Romano*, 7 September 2019, p. 8.

[225] *Arrival Ceremony*, Colombo, Sri Lanka (13 January 2015): *L'Osservatore Romano*, 14 January 2015, p. 7.

[226] *Meeting with the Children of the "Bethany Centre" and Representatives of other Charitable Centres of Albania*, Tirana, Albania (21 September 2014): *Insegnamenti* II, 2 (2014), 288.

[227] *Video Message to the TED Conference in Vancouver* (26 April 2017): *L'Osservatore Romano*, 27 April 2017, p. 7.

and sins. Authentic reconciliation does not flee from conflict, but is achieved *in* conflict, resolving it through dialogue and open, honest and patient negotiation. Conflict between different groups "if it abstains from enmities and mutual hatred, gradually changes into an honest discussion of differences founded on a desire for justice."[228]

245. On numerous occasions, I have spoken of "a principle indispensable to the building of friendship in society: namely, that unity is greater than conflict... This is not to opt for a kind of syncretism, or for the absorption of one into the other, but rather for a resolution which takes place on a higher plane and preserves what is valid and useful on both sides."[229] All of us know that "when we, as individuals and communities, learn to look beyond ourselves and our particular interests, then understanding and mutual commitment bear fruit... in a setting where conflicts, tensions and even groups once considered inimical can attain a multifaceted unity that gives rise to new life."[230]

MEMORY

246. Of those who have endured much unjust and cruel suffering, a sort of "social forgiveness" must not be demanded. Reconciliation is a personal act, and no one can impose it upon an entire society, however great the need to foster it. In a strictly personal way, someone, by a free and generous decision, can choose not to demand punishment (cf. *Mt* 5:44-46), even if it is quite legitimately demanded by society and its justice system. However, it is not possible to proclaim a "blan-

---

[228] PIUS XI, Encyclical Letter *Quadragesimo Anno* (15 May 1931): AAS 23 (1931), 213.

[229] Apostolic Exhortation *Evangelii Gaudium* (24 November 2013), 228: AAS 105 (2013), 1113.

[230] *Meeting with the Civil Authorities, Civil Society and the Diplomatic Corps*, Riga, Latvia (24 September 2018): *L'Osservatore Romano*, 24-25 September 2018, p. 7.

ket reconciliation" in an effort to bind wounds by decree or to cover injustices in a cloak of oblivion. Who can claim the right to forgive in the name of others? It is moving to see forgiveness shown by those who are able to leave behind the harm they suffered, but it is also humanly understandable in the case of those who cannot. In any case, forgetting is never the answer.

247. The *Shoah* must not be forgotten. It is "the enduring symbol of the depths to which human evil can sink when, spurred by false ideologies, it fails to recognize the fundamental dignity of each person, which merits unconditional respect regardless of ethnic origin or religious belief."[231] As I think of it, I cannot help but repeat this prayer: "Lord, remember us in your mercy. Grant us the grace to be ashamed of what we men have done, to be ashamed of this massive idolatry, of having despised and destroyed our own flesh which you formed from the earth, to which you gave life with your own breath of life. Never again, Lord, never again!."[232]

248. Nor must we forget the atomic bombs dropped on Hiroshima and Nagasaki. Once again, "I pay homage to all the victims, and I bow before the strength and dignity of those who, having survived those first moments, for years afterward bore in the flesh immense suffering, and in their spirit seeds of death that drained their vital energy... We cannot allow present and future generations to lose the memory of what happened. It is a memory that ensures and encourages the building of a more fair and fraternal future."[233] Neither must we forget the persecutions, the slave trade and the ethnic killings that continue in various countries, as well as the many other historical

---

[231] *Arrival Ceremony*, Tel Aviv, Israel (25 May 2014): *Insegnamenti* II, 1 (2014), 604.

[232] *Visit to the Yad Vashem Memorial*, Jerusalem (26 May 2014): AAS 106 (2014), 228.

[233] *Address at the Peace Memorial*, Hiroshima, Japan (24 November 2019): *L'Osservatore Romano*, 25-26 November 2019, p. 8.

events that make us ashamed of our humanity. They need to be remembered, always and ever anew. We must never grow accustomed or inured to them.

249. Nowadays, it is easy to be tempted to turn the page, to say that all these things happened long ago and we should look to the future. For God's sake, no! We can never move forward without remembering the past; we do not progress without an honest and unclouded memory. We need to "keep alive the flame of collective conscience, bearing witness to succeeding generations to the horror of what happened," because that witness "awakens and preserves the memory of the victims, so that the conscience of humanity may rise up in the face of every desire for dominance and destruction."[234] The victims themselves – individuals, social groups or nations – need to do so, lest they succumb to the mindset that leads to justifying reprisals and every kind of violence in the name of the great evil endured. For this reason, I think not only of the need to remember the atrocities, but also all those who, amid such great inhumanity and corruption, retained their dignity and, with gestures small or large, chose the part of solidarity, forgiveness and fraternity. To remember goodness is also a healthy thing.

Forgiving but not forgetting

250. Forgiving does not mean forgetting. Or better, in the face of a reality that can in no way be denied, relativized or concealed, forgiveness is still possible. In the face of an action that can never be tolerated, justified or excused, we can still forgive. In the face of something that cannot be forgotten for any reason, we can still forgive. Free and heartfelt forgiveness is something noble, a reflection of God's own infinite ability to forgive. If forgiveness is gratuitous, then it can be

---

[234] *Message for the 2020 World Day of Peace* (8 December 2019), 2: *L'Osservatore Romano*, 13 December 2019, p. 8.

shown even to someone who resists repentance and is unable to beg pardon.

251. Those who truly forgive do not forget. Instead, they choose not to yield to the same destructive force that caused them so much suffering. They break the vicious circle; they halt the advance of the forces of destruction. They choose not to spread in society the spirit of revenge that will sooner or later return to take its toll. Revenge never truly satisfies victims. Some crimes are so horrendous and cruel that the punishment of those who perpetrated them does not serve to repair the harm done. Even killing the criminal would not be enough, nor could any form of torture prove commensurate with the sufferings inflicted on the victim. Revenge resolves nothing.

252. This does not mean impunity. Justice is properly sought solely out of love of justice itself, out of respect for the victims, as a means of preventing new crimes and protecting the common good, not as an alleged outlet for personal anger. Forgiveness is precisely what enables us to pursue justice without falling into a spiral of revenge or the injustice of forgetting.

253. When injustices have occurred on both sides, it is important to take into clear account whether they were equally grave or in any way comparable. Violence perpetrated by the state, using its structures and power, is not on the same level as that perpetrated by particular groups. In any event, one cannot claim that the unjust sufferings of one side alone should be commemorated. The Bishops of Croatia have stated that, "we owe equal respect to every innocent victim. There can be no racial, national, confessional or partisan differences."[235]

254. I ask God "to prepare our hearts to encounter our brothers and sisters, so that we may overcome our differences rooted in

---

[235] CROATIAN BISHOPS' CONFERENCE, *Letter on the Fiftieth Anniversary of the End of the Second World War* (1 May 1995).

political thinking, language, culture and religion. Let us ask him to anoint our whole being with the balm of his mercy, which heals the injuries caused by mistakes, misunderstandings and disputes. And let us ask him for the grace to send us forth, in humility and meekness, along the demanding but enriching path of seeking peace."[236]

WAR AND THE DEATH PENALTY

255. There are two extreme situations that may come to be seen as solutions in especially dramatic circumstances, without realizing that they are false answers that do not resolve the problems they are meant to solve and ultimately do no more than introduce new elements of destruction in the fabric of national and global society. These are war and the death penalty.

The injustice of war

256. "Deceit is in the mind of those who plan evil, but those who counsel peace have joy" (*Prov* 12:20). Yet there are those who seek solutions in war, frequently fueled by a breakdown in relations, hegemonic ambitions, abuses of power, fear of others and a tendency to see diversity as an obstacle.[237] War is not a ghost from the past but a constant threat. Our world is encountering growing difficulties on the slow path to peace upon which it had embarked and which had already begun to bear good fruit.

257. Since conditions that favour the outbreak of wars are once again increasing, I can only reiterate that "war is the negation of all rights and a dramatic assault on the environment. If we want

---

[236] *Homily*, Amman, Jordan (24 May 2014): *Insegnamenti* II, 1 (2014), 593.

[237] Cf. *Message for the 2020 World Day of Peace* (8 December 2019), 1: *L'Osservatore Romano*, 13 December 2019, p. 8.

true integral human development for all, we must work tire-lessly to avoid war between nations and peoples. To this end, there is a need to ensure the uncontested rule of law and tireless recourse to negotiation, mediation and arbitration, as proposed by the *Charter of the United Nations*, which constitutes truly a fundamental juridical norm."[238] The seventy-five years since the establishment of the United Nations and the experience of the first twenty years of this millennium have shown that the full application of international norms proves truly effective, and that failure to comply with them is detrimental. The *Charter of the United Nations*, when observed and applied with transparency and sincerity, is an obligatory reference point of justice and a channel of peace. Here there can be no room for disguising false intentions or placing the partisan interests of one country or group above the global common good. If rules are considered simply as means to be used whenever it proves advantageous, and to be ignored when it is not, uncontrollable forces are unleashed that cause grave harm to societies, to the poor and vulnerable, to fraternal relations, to the environment and to cultural treasures, with irretrievable losses for the global community.

258. War can easily be chosen by invoking all sorts of alleg-edly humanitarian, defensive or precautionary excuses, and even resorting to the manipulation of information. In recent decades, every single war has been ostensibly "justified." The *Catechism of the Catholic Church* speaks of the possibil-ity of legitimate *defence* by means of military force, which involves demonstrating that certain "rigorous conditions of moral legitimacy"[239] have been met. Yet it is easy to fall into an overly broad interpretation of this potential right. In this way, some would also wrongly justify even "preventive" at-tacks or acts of war that can hardly avoid entailing "evils and

---

[238] *Address to the Members of the General Assembly of the United Nations*, New York (25 September 2015): AAS 107 (2015), 1041-1042.
[239] No. 2309.

disorders graver than the evil to be eliminated."[240] At issue is whether the development of nuclear, chemical and biological weapons, and the enormous and growing possibilities offered by new technologies, have granted war an uncontrollable destructive power over great numbers of innocent civilians. The truth is that "never has humanity had such power over itself, yet nothing ensures that it will be used wisely."[241] We can no longer think of war as a solution, because its risks will probably always be greater than its supposed benefits. In view of this, it is very difficult nowadays to invoke the rational criteria elaborated in earlier centuries to speak of the possibility of a "just war." Never again war![242]

259. It should be added that, with increased globalization, what might appear as an immediate or practical solution for one part of the world initiates a chain of violent and often latent effects that end up harming the entire planet and opening the way to new and worse wars in the future. In today's world, there are no longer just isolated outbreaks of war in one country or another; instead, we are experiencing a "world war fought piecemeal," since the destinies of countries are so closely interconnected on the global scene.

260. In the words of Saint John XXIII, "it no longer makes sense to maintain that war is a fit instrument with which to repair the violation of justice."[243] In making this point amid great international tension, he voiced the growing desire for peace emerging in the Cold War period. He supported the conviction

---

[240] Ibid.

[241] Encyclical Letter *Laudato Si'* (24 May 2015), 104: AAS 107 (2015), 888.

[242] Saint Augustine, who forged a concept of "just war" that we no longer uphold in our own day, also said that "it is a higher glory still to stay war itself with a word, than to slay men with the sword, and to procure or maintain peace by peace, not by war" (*Epistola* 229, 2: PL 33, 1020).

[243] Encyclical Letter *Pacem in Terris* (11 April 1963): AAS 55 (1963), 291.

that the arguments for peace are stronger than any calculation of particular interests and confidence in the use of weaponry. The opportunities offered by the end of the Cold War were not, however, adequately seized due to a lack of a vision for the future and a shared consciousness of our common destiny. Instead, it proved easier to pursue partisan interests without upholding the universal common good. The dread spectre of war thus began to gain new ground.

261. Every war leaves our world worse than it was before. War is a failure of politics and of humanity, a shameful capitulation, a stinging defeat before the forces of evil. Let us not remain mired in theoretical discussions, but touch the wounded flesh of the victims. Let us look once more at all those civilians whose killing was considered "collateral damage." Let us ask the victims themselves. Let us think of the refugees and displaced, those who suffered the effects of atomic radiation or chemical attacks, the mothers who lost their children, and the boys and girls maimed or deprived of their childhood. Let us hear the true stories of these victims of violence, look at reality through their eyes, and listen with an open heart to the stories they tell. In this way, we will be able to grasp the abyss of evil at the heart of war. Nor will it trouble us to be deemed naive for choosing peace.

262. Rules by themselves will not suffice if we continue to think that the solution to current problems is deterrence through fear or the threat of nuclear, chemical or biological weapons. Indeed, "if we take into consideration the principal threats to peace and security with their many dimensions in this multipolar world of the twenty-first century as, for example, terrorism, asymmetrical conflicts, cybersecurity, environmental problems, poverty, not a few doubts arise regarding the inadequacy of nuclear deterrence as an effective response to such challenges. These concerns are even greater when we consider the catastrophic humanitarian and environmental consequences

that would follow from any use of nuclear weapons, with devastating, indiscriminate and uncontainable effects, over time and space... We need also to ask ourselves how sustainable is a stability based on fear, when it actually increases fear and undermines relationships of trust between peoples. International peace and stability cannot be based on a false sense of security, on the threat of mutual destruction or total annihilation, or on simply maintaining a balance of power... In this context, the ultimate goal of the total elimination of nuclear weapons becomes both a challenge and a moral and humanitarian imperative... Growing interdependence and globalization mean that any response to the threat of nuclear weapons should be collective and concerted, based on mutual trust. This trust can be built only through dialogue that is truly directed to the common good and not to the protection of veiled or particular interests."[244] With the money spent on weapons and other military expenditures, let us establish a global fund[245] that can finally put an end to hunger and favour development in the most impoverished countries, so that their citizens will not resort to violent or illusory solutions, or have to leave their countries in order to seek a more dignified life.

The death penalty

263. There is yet another way to eliminate others, one aimed not at countries but at individuals. It is the death penalty. Saint John Paul II stated clearly and firmly that the death penalty is inadequate from a moral standpoint and no longer necessary from that of penal justice.[246] There can be no stepping back

---

[244] *Message to the United Nations Conference to Negotiate a Legally Binding Instrument to Prohibit Nuclear Weapons* (23 March 2017): AAS 109 (2017), 394-396.

[245] Cf. SAINT PAUL VI, Encyclical Letter *Populorum Progressio* (26 March 1967): AAS 59 (1967), 282.

[246] Cf. Encyclical Letter *Evangelium Vitae* (25 March 1995), 56: AAS 87 (1995), 463-464.

from this position. Today we state clearly that "the death penalty is inadmissible"[247] and the Church is firmly committed to calling for its abolition worldwide.[248]

264. In the New Testament, while individuals are asked not to take justice into their own hands (cf. *Rom* 12:17.19), there is also a recognition of the need for authorities to impose penalties on evildoers (cf. *Rom* 13:4; *1 Pet* 2:14). Indeed, "civic life, structured around an organized community, needs rules of coexistence, the wilful violation of which demands appropriate redress."[249] This means that legitimate public authority can and must "inflict punishments according to the seriousness of the crimes"[250] and that judicial power be guaranteed a "necessary independence in the realm of law."[251]

265. From the earliest centuries of the Church, some were clearly opposed to capital punishment. Lactantius, for example, held that "there ought to be no exception at all; that it is always unlawful to put a man to death."[252] Pope Nicholas I urged that efforts be made "to free from the punishment of death not only each of the innocent, but all the guilty as well."[253] During the trial of the murderers of two priests, Saint Augustine asked the

[247] *Address on the Twenty-fifth Anniversary of the Promulgation of the Catechism of the Catholic Church* (11 October 2017): AAS 109 (2017), 1196.

[248] Cf. CONGREGATION FOR THE DOCTRINE OF THE FAITH, *Letter to the Bishops Regarding the Revision of No. 2267 of the Catechism of the Catholic Church on the Death Penalty* (1 August 2018): *L'Osservatore Romano*, 3 August 2018, p. 8.

[249] *Address to Delegates of the International Association of Penal Law* (23 October 2014): AAS 106 (2014), 840.

[250] PONTIFICAL COUNCIL FOR JUSTICE AND PEACE, *Compendium of the Social Doctrine of the Church*, 402.

[251] SAINT JOHN PAUL II, *Address to the National Association of Magistrates* (31 March 2000), 4: AAS 92 (2000), 633.

[252] *Divinae Institutiones* VI, 20, 17: PL 6, 708.

[253] *Epistola 97 (Responsa ad consulta Bulgarorum)*, 25: PL 119, 991. "ipsi (Christo) non solum innoxios quosque, verum etiam et noxios a mortis exitio satagite cunctos eruere...."

judge not to take the life of the assassins with this argument: "We do not object to your depriving these wicked men of the freedom to commit further crimes. Our desire is rather that justice be satisfied without the taking of their lives or the maiming of their bodies in any part. And, at the same time, that by the coercive measures provided by the law, they be turned from their irrational fury to the calmness of men of sound mind, and from their evil deeds to some useful employment. This too is considered a condemnation, but who does not see that, when savage violence is restrained and remedies meant to produce repentance are provided, it should be considered a benefit rather than a mere punitive measure… Do not let the atrocity of their sins feed a desire for vengeance, but desire instead to heal the wounds which those deeds have inflicted on their souls."[254]

266. Fear and resentment can easily lead to viewing punishment in a vindictive and even cruel way, rather than as part of a process of healing and reintegration into society. Nowadays, "in some political sectors and certain media, public and private violence and revenge are incited, not only against those responsible for committing crimes, but also against those suspected, whether proven or not, of breaking the law… There is at times a tendency to deliberately fabricate enemies: stereotyped figures who represent all the characteristics that society perceives or interprets as threatening. The mechanisms that form these images are the same that allowed the spread of racist ideas in their time."[255] This has made all the more dangerous the growing practice in some countries of resorting to preventive custody, imprisonment without trial and especially the death penalty.

267. Here I would stress that "it is impossible to imagine that states today have no other means than capital punishment to protect the lives of other people from the unjust aggressor."

---

[254] *Epistola ad Marcellinum* 133, 1.2: PL 33, 509.
[255] *Address to Delegates of the International Association of Penal Law* (23 October 2014): AAS 106 (2014), 840-841.

Particularly serious in this regard are so-called extrajudicial or extralegal executions, which are "homicides deliberately committed by certain states and by their agents, often passed off as clashes with criminals or presented as the unintended consequences of the reasonable, necessary and proportionate use of force in applying the law."[256]

268. "The arguments against the death penalty are numerous and well-known. The Church has rightly called attention to several of these, such as the possibility of judicial error and the use made of such punishment by totalitarian and dictatorial regimes as a means of suppressing political dissidence or persecuting religious and cultural minorities, all victims whom the legislation of those regimes consider 'delinquents.' All Christians and people of good will are today called to work not only for the abolition of the death penalty, legal or illegal, in all its forms, but also to work for the improvement of prison conditions, out of respect for the human dignity of persons deprived of their freedom. I would link this to life imprisonment... A life sentence is a secret death penalty."[257]

269. Let us keep in mind that "not even a murderer loses his personal dignity, and God himself pledges to guarantee this."[258] The firm rejection of the death penalty shows to what extent it is possible to recognize the inalienable dignity of every human being and to accept that he or she has a place in this universe. If I do not deny that dignity to the worst of criminals, I will not deny it to anyone. I will give everyone the possibility of sharing this planet with me, despite all our differences.

270. I ask Christians who remain hesitant on this point, and those tempted to yield to violence in any form, to keep in mind

---

[256] Ibid., 842.

[257] Ibid.

[258] SAINT JOHN PAUL II, Encyclical Letter *Evangelium Vitae* (25 March 1995), 9: AAS 87 (1995), 411.

the words of the book of Isaiah: "They shall beat their swords into plowshares" (2:4). For us, this prophecy took flesh in Christ Jesus who, seeing a disciple tempted to violence, said firmly: "Put your sword back into its place; for all who take the sword will perish by the sword" (*Mt* 26:52). These words echoed the ancient warning: "I will require a reckoning for human life. Whoever sheds the blood of a man, by man shall his blood be shed" (*Gen* 9:5-6). Jesus' reaction, which sprang from his heart, bridges the gap of the centuries and reaches the present as an enduring appeal.

CHAPTER EIGHT

RELIGIONS AT THE SERVICE OF FRATERNITY

IN OUR WORLD

271. The different religions, based on their respect for each human person as a creature called to be a child of God, contribute significantly to building fraternity and defending justice in society. Dialogue between the followers of different religions does not take place simply for the sake of diplomacy, consideration or tolerance. In the words of the Bishops of India, "the goal of dialogue is to establish friendship, peace and harmony, and to share spiritual and moral values and experiences in a spirit of truth and love."[259]

THE ULTIMATE FOUNDATION

272. As believers, we are convinced that, without an openness to the Father of all, there will be no solid and stable reasons for an appeal to fraternity. We are certain that "only with this awareness that we are not orphans, but children, can we live

---

[259] CATHOLIC BISHOPS' CONFERENCE OF INDIA, *Response of the Church in India to the Present-day Challenges* (9 March 2016).

in peace with one another."[260] For "reason, by itself, is capable of grasping the equality between men and of giving stability to their civic coexistence, but it cannot establish fraternity."[261]

273. In this regard, I wish to cite the following memorable statement: "If there is no transcendent truth, in obedience to which man achieves his full identity, then there is no sure principle for guaranteeing just relations between people. Their self-interest as a class, group or nation would inevitably set them in opposition to one another. If one does not acknowledge transcendent truth, then the force of power takes over, and each person tends to make full use of the means at his disposal in order to impose his own interests or his own opinion, with no regard for the rights of others… The root of modern totalitarianism is to be found in the denial of the transcendent dignity of the human person who, as the visible image of the invisible God, is therefore by his very nature the subject of rights that no one may violate – no individual, group, class, nation or state. Not even the majority of the social body may violate these rights, by going against the minority."[262]

274. From our faith experience and from the wisdom accumulated over centuries, but also from lessons learned from our many weaknesses and failures, we, the believers of the different religions, know that our witness to God benefits our societies. The effort to seek God with a sincere heart, provided it is never sullied by ideological or self-serving aims, helps us recognize one another as travelling companions, truly brothers and sisters. We are convinced that "when, in the name of an ideology, there is an attempt to remove God from a society, that society ends up adoring idols, and very soon men and women lose their way,

---

[260] *Homily at Mass in Domus Sanctae Marthae* (17 May 2020).

[261] BENEDICT XVI, Encyclical Letter *Caritas in Veritate* (29 June 2009), 19: AAS 101 (2009), 655.

[262] SAINT JOHN PAUL II, Encyclical Letter *Centesimus Annus* (1 May 1991), 44: AAS 83 (1991), 849.

their dignity is trampled and their rights violated. You know well how much suffering is caused by the denial of freedom of conscience and of religious freedom, and how that wound leaves a humanity which is impoverished, because it lacks hope and ideals to guide it."[263]

275. It should be acknowledged that "among the most important causes of the crises of the modern world are a desensitized human conscience, a distancing from religious values and the prevailing individualism accompanied by materialistic philosophies that deify the human person and introduce worldly and material values in place of supreme and transcendental principles."[264] It is wrong when the only voices to be heard in public debate are those of the powerful and "experts." Room needs to be made for reflections born of religious traditions that are the repository of centuries of experience and wisdom. For "religious classics can prove meaningful in every age; they have an enduring power ." Yet often they are viewed with disdain as a result of "the myopia of a certain rationalism."[265]

276. For these reasons, the Church, while respecting the autonomy of political life, does not restrict her mission to the private sphere. On the contrary, "she cannot and must not remain on the sidelines" in the building of a better world, or fail to "reawaken the spiritual energy" that can contribute to the betterment of society.[266] It is true that religious ministers must not engage in the party politics that are the proper domain of the laity, but neither can they renounce the political dimension

---

[263] *Address to the Leaders of Other Religions and Other Christian Denominations*, Tirana, Albania (21 September 2014): *Insegnamenti* II, 2 (2014), 277.

[264] *Document on Human Fraternity for World Peace and Living Together*, Abu Dhabi (4 February 2019): *L'Osservatore Romano*, 4-5 February 2019, p. 6.

[265] Apostolic Exhortation *Evangelii Gaudium* (24 November 2013), 256: AAS 105 (2013), 1123.

[266] BENEDICT XVI, Encyclical Letter *Deus Caritas Est* (25 December 2005), 28: AAS 98 (2006), 240.

of life itself,[267] which involves a constant attention to the common good and a concern for integral human development. The Church "has a public role over and above her charitable and educational activities." She works for "the advancement of humanity and of universal fraternity."[268] She does not claim to compete with earthly powers, but to offer herself as "a family among families, this is the Church, open to bearing witness in today's world, open to faith hope and love for the Lord and for those whom he loves with a preferential love. A home with open doors. The Church is a home with open doors, because she is a mother."[269] And in imitation of Mary, the Mother of Jesus, "we want to be a Church that serves, that leaves home and goes forth from its places of worship, goes forth from its sacristies, in order to accompany life, to sustain hope, to be the sign of unity... to build bridges, to break down walls, to sow seeds of reconciliation."[270]

Christian identity

277. The Church esteems the ways in which God works in other religions, and "rejects nothing of what is true and holy in these religions. She has a high regard for their manner of life and conduct, their precepts and doctrines which... often reflect a ray of that truth which enlightens all men and women."[271] Yet we Christians are very much aware that "if the music of the Gospel ceases to resonate in our very being, we will lose the joy born of compassion, the tender love born of trust, the capacity for reconciliation that has its source in our knowledge that we

---

[267] "Man is a political animal," ARISTOTLE, *Politics*, 1253a 1-3.

[268] BENEDICT XVI, Encyclical Letter *Caritas in Veritate* (29 June 2009), 11: AAS 101 (2009), 648.

[269] *Address to the Catholic Community*, Rakovski, Bulgaria (6 May 2019): *L'Osservatore Romano*, 8 May 2019, p. 9.

[270] *Homily*, Santiago de Cuba (22 September 2015): AAS 107 (2015), 1005.

[271] SECOND VATICAN ECUMENICAL COUNCIL, Declaration on the Relation of the Church to Non-Christian Religions *Nostra Aetate*, 2.

have been forgiven and sent forth. If the music of the Gospel ceases to sound in our homes, our public squares, our workplaces, our political and financial life, then we will no longer hear the strains that challenge us to defend the dignity of every man and woman."[272] Others drink from other sources. For us the wellspring of human dignity and fraternity is in the Gospel of Jesus Christ. From it, there arises, "for Christian thought and for the action of the Church, the primacy given to relationship, to the encounter with the sacred mystery of the other, to universal communion with the entire human family, as a vocation of all."[273]

278. Called to take root in every place, the Church has been present for centuries throughout the world, for that is what it means to be "catholic." She can thus understand, from her own experience of grace and sin, the beauty of the invitation to universal love. Indeed, "all things human are our concern... wherever the councils of nations come together to establish the rights and duties of man, we are honoured to be permitted to take our place among them."[274] For many Christians, this journey of fraternity also has a Mother, whose name is Mary. Having received this universal motherhood at the foot of the cross (cf. *Jn* 19:26), she cares not only for Jesus but also for "the rest of her children" (cf. *Rev* 12:17). In the power of the risen Lord, she wants to give birth to a new world, where all of us are brothers and sisters, where there is room for all those whom our societies discard, where justice and peace are resplendent.

279. We Christians ask that, in those countries where we are a minority, we be guaranteed freedom, even as we ourselves promote that freedom for non-Christians in places where they are a

---

[272] *Ecumenical Prayer Service*, Riga, Latvia (24 September 2018): *L'Osservatore Romano*, 24-25 September 2018, p. 8.

[273] *Lectio Divina*, Pontifical Lateran University, Rome (26 March 2019): *L'Osservatore Romano*, 27 March 2019, p. 10.

[274] SAINT PAUL VI, Encyclical Letter *Ecclesiam Suam* (6 August 1964): AAS 56 (1964), 650.

minority. One fundamental human right must not be forgotten in the journey towards fraternity and peace. It is religious freedom for believers of all religions. That freedom proclaims that we can "build harmony and understanding between different cultures and religions. It also testifies to the fact that, since the important things we share are so many, it is possible to find a means of serene, ordered and peaceful coexistence, accepting our differences and rejoicing that, as children of the one God, we are all brothers and sisters."[275]

280. At the same time, we ask God to strengthen unity within the Church, a unity enriched by differences reconciled by the working of the Spirit. For "in the one Spirit we were all baptized into one body" (*1 Cor* 12:13), in which each member has his or her distinctive contribution to make. As Saint Augustine said, "the ear sees through the eye, and the eye hears through the ear."[276] It is also urgent to continue to bear witness to the journey of encounter between the different Christian confessions. We cannot forget Christ's desire "that they may all be one" (cf. *Jn* 17:21). Hearing his call, we recognize with sorrow that the process of globalization still lacks the prophetic and spiritual contribution of unity among Christians. This notwithstanding, "even as we make this journey towards full communion, we already have the duty to offer common witness to the love of God for all people by working together in the service of humanity."[277]

RELIGION AND VIOLENCE

281. A journey of peace is possible between religions. Its point of departure must be God's way of seeing things. "God does

---

[275] *Address to the Civil Authorities*, Bethlehem, Palestine (25 May 2014): *Insegnamenti* II, 1 (2014), 597.

[276] *Enarrationes in Psalmos*, 130, 6: PL 37, 1707.

[277] *Common Declaration of Pope Francis and Ecumenical Patriarch Bartholomew*, Jerusalem (25 May 2014), 5: *L'Osservatore Romano*, 26-27 May 2014, p. 6.

not see with his eyes, God sees with his heart. And God's love is the same for everyone, regardless of religion. Even if they are atheists, his love is the same. When the last day comes, and there is sufficient light to see things as they really are, we are going to find ourselves quite surprised."[278]

282. It follows that "we believers need to find occasions to speak with one another and to act together for the common good and the promotion of the poor. This has nothing to do with watering down or concealing our deepest convictions when we encounter others who think differently than ourselves... For the deeper, stronger and richer our own identity is, the more we will be capable of enriching others with our own proper contribution."[279] We believers are challenged to return to our sources, in order to concentrate on what is essential: worship of God and love for our neighbour, lest some of our teachings, taken out of context, end up feeding forms of contempt, hatred, xenophobia or negation of others. The truth is that violence has no basis in our fundamental religious convictions, but only in their distortion.

283. Sincere and humble worship of God "bears fruit not in discrimination, hatred and violence, but in respect for the sacredness of life, respect for the dignity and freedom of others, and loving commitment to the welfare of all."[280] Truly, "whoever does not love does not know God, for God is love" (*1 Jn* 4:8). For this reason, "terrorism is deplorable and threatens the security of people – be they in the East or the West, the North or the South – and disseminates panic, terror and pessimism, but this is not due to religion, even when terrorists instrumentalize it. It is due, rather, to an accumulation

---

[278] From the film *Pope Francis: A Man of His Word*, by Wim Wenders (2018).

[279] Post-Synodal Apostolic Exhortation *Querida Amazonia* (2 February 2020), 106.

[280] *Homily*, Colombo, Sri Lanka (14 January 2015): AAS 107 (2015), 139.

of incorrect interpretations of religious texts and to policies linked to hunger, poverty, injustice, oppression and pride. That is why it is so necessary to stop supporting terrorist movements fuelled by financing, the provision of weapons and strategy, and by attempts to justify these movements, even using the media. All these must be regarded as international crimes that threaten security and world peace. Such terrorism must be condemned in all its forms and expressions."[281] Religious convictions about the sacred meaning of human life permit us "to recognize the fundamental values of our common humanity, values in the name of which we can and must cooperate, build and dialogue, pardon and grow; this will allow different voices to unite in creating a melody of sublime nobility and beauty, instead of fanatical cries of hatred."[282]

284. At times fundamentalist violence is unleashed in some groups, of whatever religion, by the rashness of their leaders. Yet, "the commandment of peace is inscribed in the depths of the religious traditions that we represent... As religious leaders, we are called to be true 'people of dialogue,' to cooperate in building peace not as intermediaries but as authentic mediators. Intermediaries seek to give everyone a discount, ultimately in order to gain something for themselves. The mediator, on the other hand, is one who retains nothing for himself, but rather spends himself generously until he is consumed, knowing that the only gain is peace. Each one of us is called to be an artisan of peace, by uniting and not dividing, by extinguishing hatred and not holding on to it, by opening paths of dialogue and not by constructing new walls."[283]

---

[281] *Document on Human Fraternity for World Peace and Living Together,* Abu Dhabi (4 February 2019): *L'Osservatore Romano,* 4-5 February 2019, p. 7.
[282] *Address to Civil Authorities,* Sarajevo, Bosnia-Herzegovina (6 June 2015): *L'Osservatore Romano,* 7 June 2015, p. 7.
[283] *Address to the International Meeting for Peace organized by the Community of Sant'Egidio* (30 September 2013): *Insegnamenti* I, 1 (2013), 301-302.

An appeal

285. In my fraternal meeting, which I gladly recall, with the Grand Imam Ahmad Al-Tayyeb, "we resolutely that religions must never incite war, hateful attitudes, hostility and extremism, nor must they incite violence or the shedding of blood. These tragic realities are the consequence of a deviation from religious teachings. They result from a political manipulation of religions and from interpretations made by religious groups who, in the course of history, have taken advantage of the power of religious sentiment in the hearts of men and women... God, the Almighty, has no need to be defended by anyone and does not want his name to be used to terrorize people."[284] For this reason I would like to reiterate here the appeal for peace, justice and fraternity that we made together:

"In the name of God, who has created all human beings equal in rights, duties and dignity, and who has called them to live together as brothers and sisters, to fill the earth and make known the values of goodness, love and peace;

"In the name of innocent human life that God has forbidden to kill, affirming that whoever kills a person is like one who kills the whole of humanity, and that whoever saves a person is like one who saves the whole of humanity;

"In the name of the poor, the destitute, the marginalized and those most in need, whom God has commanded us to help as a duty required of all persons, especially the wealthy and those of means;

"In the name of orphans, widows, refugees and those exiled from their homes and their countries; in the name of all victims

---

[284] *Document on Human Fraternity for World Peace and Living Together*, Abu Dhabi (4 February 2019): *L'Osservatore Romano*, 4-5 February 2019, p. 6.

of wars, persecution and injustice; in the name of the weak, those who live in fear, prisoners of war and those tortured in any part of the world, without distinction;

"In the name of peoples who have lost their security, peace and the possibility of living together, becoming victims of destruction, calamity and war;

"In the name of *human fraternity*, that embraces all human beings, unites them and renders them equal;

"In the name of this *fraternity* torn apart by policies of extremism and division, by systems of unrestrained profit or by hateful ideological tendencies that manipulate the actions and the future of men and women;

"In the name of freedom, that God has given to all human beings, creating them free and setting them apart by this gift;

"In the name of justice and mercy, the foundations of prosperity and the cornerstone of faith;

"In the name of all persons of goodwill present in every part of the world;

"In the name of God and of everything stated thus far, declare the adoption of a culture of dialogue as the path; mutual cooperation as the code of conduct; reciprocal understanding as the method and standard."[285]

* * *

286. In these pages of reflection on universal fraternity, I felt inspired particularly by Saint Francis of Assisi, but also by others of our brothers and sisters who are not Catholics: Martin

---

[285] Ibid.

Luther King, Desmond Tutu, Mahatma Gandhi and many more. Yet I would like to conclude by mentioning another person of deep faith who, drawing upon his intense experience of God, made a journey of transformation towards feeling a brother to all. I am speaking of Blessed Charles de Foucauld.

287. Blessed Charles directed his ideal of total surrender to God towards an identification with the poor, abandoned in the depths of the African desert. In that setting, he expressed his desire to feel himself a brother to every human being,[286] and asked a friend to "pray to God that I truly be the brother of all."[287] He wanted to be, in the end, "the universal brother."[288] Yet only by identifying with the least did he come at last to be the brother of all. May God inspire that dream in each one of us. Amen.

A Prayer to the Creator

Lord, Father of our human family,
you created all human beings equal in dignity:
pour forth into our hearts a fraternal spirit
and inspire in us a dream of renewed encounter.,
dialogue, justice and peace.
Move us to create healthier societies
and a more dignified world,
a world without hunger, poverty, violence and war.

May our hearts be open
to all the peoples and nations of the earth.
May we recognize the goodness and beauty that you have
sown in each of us,

---

[286] Cf. CHARLES DE FOUCAULD, *Méditation sur le Notre Père* (23 January 1897).

[287] *Letter to Henry de Castries* (29 November 1901).

[288] *Letter to Madame de Bondy* (7 January 1902). Saint Paul VI used these words in praising his commitment: Encyclical Letter *Populorum Progressio* (26 March 1967): AAS 59 (1967), 263.

and thus forge bonds of unity, common projects,
and shared dreams. Amen.

An Ecumenical Christian Prayer

O God, Trinity of love,
from the profound communion of your divine life,
pour out upon us a torrent of fraternal love.
Grant us the love reflected in the actions of Jesus,
in his family of Nazareth,
and in the early Christian community.

Grant that we Christians may live the Gospel,
discovering Christ in each human being,
recognizing him crucified
in the sufferings of the abandoned
and forgotten of our world,
and risen in each brother or sister
who makes a new start.

Come, Holy Spirit, show us your beauty,
reflected in all the peoples of the earth,
so that we may discover anew
that all are important and all are necessary,
different faces of the one humanity
that God so loves. Amen.

*Given in Assisi, at the tomb of Saint Francis, on 3 October,
Vigil of the Feast of the Saint, in the year 2020, the eighth of
my Pontificate.*

Franciscus

Made in the USA
Las Vegas, NV
14 January 2021